JEROME ODLUM

EACH
DAWN
I DIE

The
BOBBS-MERRILL COMPANY
Publishers
INDIANAPOLIS • NEW YORK

To WILLIAM H. AMESBURY

Minneapolis and St. Paul newspaper and
magazine publisher, who, for the last
three years, has been my boss, my friend,
my adviser and my critic.

Each dawn I die,
And as the morning
Stars retreat,
So does my heart stop,
Beat by beat. . . .

SAM H. KAUFMAN

1

WE ARE just starting across the prison yard when Stacey halts us. His face is the usual emotionless mask, but all the fires of a thousand hates are burning in his eyes.

I ask, "What's up?"

"Ludke and Carlisle just ratted on me."

Mueller demands, "What about?"

"Soda. They snitched to the deputy warden."

Mueller kicks at the fresh spring grass.

Lassiter says, "It'll probably mean the hole."

Stacey nods.

Soda—sodium bicarbonate, common baking soda—is contraband in Stony Point prison. Some of the inmates use it to make snuff—a teaspoonful and a pinch of salt to a can of dampened, powdered tobacco—and snuff is forbidden. If we're caught with either snuff or soda, we get ten days in the hole on bread and water. Consequently, soda is dangerous stuff to monkey with, and a tobacco can full brings five dollars in merchandise. Some of the inmate nurses and the kitchen help have access to the soda supply, and a few of the screws smuggle it in and trade it to the inmates for shoes or tobacco or fountain pens.

11

Mueller growls, "What'd you let those rats know you had the stuff for?"

"Let them know!" cries Stacey. "Do you think I'm nuts? They saw Garsky slip it to me this morning at sick call. Then as soon as we hit the yard this afternoon, the rats bee-lined for Deputy Armstrong. After they'd talked to him for a minute, he ran me down and frisked me."

Mueller asks, "Did he find the stuff on you?"

"Hell, no. I wouldn't carry that stuff around. It's hidden up in my cell—hanging down the ventilator shaft on a piece of string."

Lassiter says, "Do you figure he's up there shaking down your cell now?"

Stacey shrugs. "I don't know, but if he is, and if he starts fishing around in the shaft, I'm a blowed-up sucker."

"One of these days," mutters Mueller, "those rats'll snitch on the wrong party. They haven't been around here more than a month, but they're overdue for about ten or twelve inches of shiv in the guts already."

Stacey makes no reply. He is a small, silent man with a face like a mask of sallow parchment. Only his eyes betray him during moments of anger. . . . Little is known of his past, save what has appeared in the newspapers and what is repeated from fancy. I am a former newspaperman, and have worked beside him daily during the three months since I was framed into Stony Point, but he has told me almost nothing about himself that hadn't already come over the press wires before his arrest two years ago. Stacey was always swell copy, but the only thing I can write about him after I get out of here is that he started out in life as a professional knife-thrower with a circus or a carnival. . . . Whatever he's thinking about at the present, he usually keeps to himself.

The regular Saturday afternoon baseball game between the prison team and a scrub outfit from the county seat gets under way and sets the inmates to howling. But we four have lost all interest in the game, don't even drift toward the sidelines. The threat of the hole, a menace that hangs perpetually above us, is about to materialize for Stacey.

Then Garsky, the inmate who gave Stacey the soda, joins us. He is known among the convicts here as a solid party and is well liked, even though he is a little windy. Rumor has it that before Stacey's imprisonment, Garsky was a lieutenant of his on the outside. Since the pair have been here together, they've been inseparable. . . . Garsky talks a lot, but when he's all through you realize he's said nothing he didn't want you to hear. When I first came here, I tried to pump him for inside information that I might use in a feature story after I get out, but I learned little that couldn't be found in the published biography of any crook.

Garsky asks, "Why the long faces, and why ain'tcha watching the game?"

Mueller comments obscenely on where they can put their game, and tells Stacey's story.

"Oh, the finks!" howls Garsky. "The dirty, low-born rats!"

"Don't worry, Garsky," says Stacey. "If there's any rap to take on this, I'm taking it alone."

Mueller snarls, "If some of us had the guts of a sheep, we'd've bumped those snitching punks the day they came here, and there'd be no raps for anybody to take."

"It's too tough," says Garsky. "The rats've got us beat right from the start. Anybody shoves a knife in either one of them and it means the book in the hole."

"I'm not so sure of that," says Stacey.

"Plenty of us've started out to bump them," rumbles Mueller, "and then didn't dare go through with it."

"That's just it," snorts Garsky. "That's where the rats've got us beat. Take right now, for instance. We sound off about what we're gonna do, not paying any attention to who might be walking by and listening, and the first thing you know, the rats've got ahold of it. After that, you might as well put it in the paper. . . . It's just like I've always said: if you're gonna bump a guy, don't tell nobody—not even yourself. Then there ain't no witnesses."

"The right kind of witnesses are just what you'd need," observes Mueller. "They'd alibi you till hell wouldn't have it."

Garsky is silent for a moment. And then, "By God, you're right! Funny I never thought of that angle before. Most of these guys'd be blind, deaf and dumb if somebody got rid of the rats for them. Trouble is, the joint's full of them."

"The way to do it," says Mueller, "would be for one man, or maybe two, to plan it all out just between themselves, then do it before the rest of the rats got wind of it. Then maybe there wouldn't be any snitching around here for awhile, and a guy could shake time a little easier."

"Sure," says Garsky. "I remember once in Joliet when a rat got heaved off the fourth gallery. Fifty guys were marching to their cells. They bunched up a little so the screw at the end of the cell hall couldn't see what was up. After it was over, nobody saw nothing, except the guys closest to him said it looked like he tripped and rolled under the railing . . . Christ, how he yelled when they heaved him overboard!"

"Yeah," says Mueller. "Those rats are all the same. Big-shot, hot-stuff on the outside. Kill anybody for a dime, providing the other guy isn't looking. Then as soon as they're caught, they start ratting all over the joint."

Ludke and Carlisle, supposedly a couple of hot-shot gunmen from the East, were sent to Stony Point about a month ago and hadn't been here two days before they started ratting every time they saw an inmate break a rule. . . . They should have been given life sentences for first degree murder, but especially good legal talent, plus a strong political pull that no one can explain, got them off with five-year sentences for manslaughter after they'd been paid to pull an insurance murder in my home town. The prosecutor, according to rumor, exerted little effort to imprison them for any

length of time, accepting, instead, their plea of guilty
providing they'd be sentenced to no more than five
years. The man who paid them to commit the killing
was found hanged in the county jail. The affair was
hushed and branded a suicide, but Joe Campbell, my
old editor, believes that Ludke and Carlisle killed the
man to stifle his testimony.

Garsky snaps his fingers, then seizes Stacey's arm.
"Come on over here," he orders. "I got something
to tell you."

"Spill it here," says Stacey wearily.

"No, this is private stuff. Come on with me. I
just got an idea."

Stacey shrugs his shoulders. "He's got another
idea."

They shuffle off toward the drinking fountain, which
lies in the shadow of the north wall. . . . Garsky is
forever getting ideas and pulling Stacey off to one side
to hear them in private. He was involved in the bank
robbery which cost Stacey his freedom, but Stacey
absolved him of any implication, the witnesses failed to
identify Garsky, and he was released without going to
trial. Later, he was trapped during the burglary of
a bank back in the mountains and given a year in Stony
Point. His time is now nearly all served and he goes
out next month. . . . Rumor adds that Garsky was
rifling the bank vault in an attempt to raise money to
help Stacey, though rumor also says that Stacey has
thousands buried on the outside. But I did once hear
Garsky say that after he's out, he'll free Stacey if it

means dynamiting the walls or running a locomotive through the solid steel gate of the railway entrance. . . . Though outwardly loud and overbearing, Garsky is loyal and true to his friends. His shrewd, calculating mind creates intricate schemes that he covers with a lot of baloney about nothing.

Mueller says, "I'm like Garsky. I've got an idea too."

Lassiter asks, "What's that?"

"I kind of think," continues Mueller slowly, "the rats snitched on the wrong party this time."

"How come?"

"Just a hunch. Stacey's plenty bad, and Garsky's no pushover. . . . That Jew'd go to hell for Stacey."

"So what happens then?" I ask.

"So they're over there figuring out an angle, and something tells me it doesn't mean any good for Ludke and Carlisle."

"Well," says Lassiter, "if that's the case, I'm glad they're over there and keeping it to themselves. I don't want in on it. I've got troubles enough, just being here."

"You and me both," I mutter.

2

SILENTLY we huddle together in the prison yard.
The past pushes itself to the surface of my mind. . . .
A little over three months ago, I was a reporter on the
Mountain Record and supported my mother and my
little brother Charles—a rôle I had filled since the death
of my father two years before. There had been a girl
too—Joyce Allen—who covered society for the same
paper. Joyce and I had gone through high school and
the university together. Then I'd got her a job with
the *Record*. All those years we'd been a part of each
other. There had never been an actual proposal, but
ever since high school days it had sort of been understood we'd marry—ever since we wrote notes to each
other in school. There was a secret process involved,
which called for lemon juice instead of ink. When
the apparently blank piece of paper was heated, the
writing showed up. We imagined it all very deep and
mysterious.

Her attempts to be of help buoyed me up through
the months that lie behind and will carry me through
whatever lies ahead. A calm, quiet girl—dark-haired,
gray-eyed and slender—she is a stalk of loveliness
which stands above the scabby realism in which I now
live. If I didn't have Joyce—if I couldn't dream of
her, think of her, plan for her—life as it is now would

not be worth the living. . . . We have been separated
only a little over three months, yet, so slow is the
passage of time in prison, it seems a thousand ages
since I was sentenced to twenty years for manslaughter—the helpless and hopelessly ensnared quarry
of the powerful political machine which I had sought
to expose.   Three months since I last felt her cheek
against mine and smelled the sweet cleanliness of her
hair and kissed her good-by. . . . At nights I lie
awake thinking of that last glimpse of her frightened
face and the hurt and pity in her eyes.

For months, we have searched through the maze of
circumstantial evidence that sent me to prison, but have
unearthed hardly a clew that may lead to proving my
innocence.   The men that put me in Stony Point knew
their business.   Every witness who appeared against
me testified honestly, telling only what he had actually
seen.   There was no perjured testimony given, for
none was needed.   The circumstances leading up to
my arrest were evidence enough in themselves.   The
Record hired good legal talent, but, as is the case when
a non-criminal becomes involved in a crime, the paper
hired lawyers versed mostly in civil law and unfamiliar
with the tricks employed by a criminal lawyer.   I saw
that my conviction was a foregone conclusion almost
before the trial got under way.   District Attorney
Hanley and his assistant Grayce were the deadly
enemies of the *Record*.   The pair prosecuted the case
with a vengeance.   The other three papers, hating our
sheet for its aggressiveness, sided with the administra-

tion; and the judge was powerless to do anything but give me the sentence prescribed by law.

It all started when Joe Campbell got wind of a graft payoff in the purchase of new police cars for the city. Joe assigned me to the story, so I got a job with the automobile firm that was supplying the cars and was suspected of bribery in the cases of four aldermen. The aldermen learned that an investigation was under way, for I'd been with the automobile firm only a couple of days when the owner rushed in one morning and asked me to help him burn the books. I was not under suspicion, for I'd been fixed with iron-clad references, so I helped him lug the company records down into the basement and throw them into the furnace. During the few days I'd been there, I had managed to pick up only a small amount of incriminating evidence—mostly circumstantial—but my part in burning the records looked like big stuff to both the paper and myself. So Joe decided I'd better stay on at the car company for a few more days to see what else I could pick up. Then we'd go ahead with the exposé and demand indictments for the aldermen and the car dealer.

I managed to worm a few more details from the salesmen, the bookkeepers and the sales manager before word came from the city hall that I was a reporter working on the story. I was kicked out of the automobile company with a warning from the owner that I'd keep my mouth shut if I knew what was good for me.

Then we broke the story all across page one, naming the aldermen and giving what details I'd picked up. The burning of the books was played up big, and I ran my version of the affair under a by-line in ten point caps.

At first, the other papers were reluctant to join us in the cry against graft, for we'd out-distanced them a mile before they even suspected what was up. The *Record* is the vigorous paper of the city, and the other sheets just naturally resented anything we unearthed that took on the appearance of a beat. But our insistent clamoring forced the grand jury to investigate, with the result that after my story had been heard, the four aldermen and the car dealer were indicted. Then the other sheets hopped on the story with a vengeance.

The night I wrote my story covering the indictments, I waited around until the city-wide edition had gone to press. I wanted to see how my version looked in print.

At about 2:30 that morning, I left the office for home. As soon as I stepped to the sidewalk, a couple of gorillas sneaked up from behind, stuck guns in my ribs, and hustled me over to my car. They didn't say a word, didn't even ask my name. I didn't get so much as a glimpse of their faces, for they marched me ahead of them.

They pushed me down on the rear floor boards of my car. As I crouched there, wondering what would come next, one of them cracked me on the head. The lights went out.

Just prior to our opening the graft inquiry, the *Record* had been crusading against drunken drivers, urging that the guilty persons be prosecuted to the full extent of the law. As a result, a drunken driver who had been involved in a fatal accident was given a thirty-year sentence for third-degree murder. He committed suicide in the county jail, but the city was still hot about drunken driving.

When I regained consciousness, it didn't take a great deal of figuring before I knew what had happened. The *Record's* drunken driving crusade had boomeranged on me. For I was soaked with whiskey, and my ears rang with the screams of dying people.

Something sharp was sticking into my side. I felt for the hurt and found the broken steering wheel half buried in the fold of my overcoat. I was in the driver's seat, alone. I put my hand on the floor board to raise myself, and cut my finger on a batch of broken glass. It accounted for the whiskey odor; the glass had been a quart of the stuff. Both the car and I were soaked with it. I could even taste it. . . . Very neatly framed.

I raised myself and peered out over the smashed dashboard into a flood of headlights. A crowd of people was outlined in the brightness, and another bunch was gathered about the wreck of my car. In the ditch across the road lay the car which mine had hit. Its trapped occupants screamed while some of the crowd sought to free them. Then the other car caught fire and there was an explosion. I can still hear the cries of horror. Four people died in those flames.

I was weak. I couldn't get out of the wreckage of my car. The steering wheel had punched a hole in my side. I was bleeding, but didn't lose consciousness again. In the light of the flames, I saw a man reach down for me. He jerked me out on the ground.

"I seen it," he said. "It was your fault. You drove over on the wrong side of the road and hit that other guy."

Then there was another voice.

"Drunk! Look at 'im—stinkin' drunk! Running around drunk, wrecking cars and killing people. Somebody watch 'im while I call the cops."

When I got to the station, I tried to tell the desk sergeant and the jailor what had happened, but they wouldn't listen.

"Go on," they growled. "You're drunk. . . . An' boy, are you gonna get it."

My arguments did no good. They refused to listen to me, merely bandaging my side and tossing me into a cell, incommunicado. I couldn't 'phone the paper or see Joyce until the paper's attorneys served a writ of habeas corpus and forced the state to file charges.

Joyce came to me as soon as I'd been arraigned and could have visitors. I asked her how bad things looked.

She shook her lovely dark head. "The other papers are playing it up big. I suppose they think this is a good time to get back at us for starting that drunken driving crusade and the graft inquiry. . . . But don't worry, darling. Everything's going to be all right.

Joe wanted me to tell you that the paper's arranging your bond now. You'll be out today."

"Do people believe I was actually driving drunk?"

She smiled and squeezed my hand. "Everybody at the office knows you were framed. They're going to clear you. So don't worry." But her face was tense, her usually serene gray eyes frightened.

I asked her what time the accident had occurred.

"Four A.M. The boys said you left the office at about 2:30, sober. I suppose the men who framed you wanted it to look as though you had plenty of time to get drunk."

Then Lew Keller and Bill Mason, a couple of reporters from our sheet, came in.

"You'll be going out on bond pretty quick, now," said Bill. "Got any idea who the birds were that took you for the ride?"

"No," I told him, "but I thought I saw Limpy Julien leaning against the building when those guys snatched me. Maybe Limpy recognized them and can give us some help."

"We'll find him," said Lew. "Once you're out we'll run this thing down in a hurry."

But they were too sanguine. I was uncertain whether I'd actually seen Limpy Julien, an ex-newsboy and long-time police character, or had merely imagined that it was he standing there by the windows which overlook the presses in the basement. And if Limpy really was there, I have no reason to believe that he noticed anything amiss or recognized the two men in

the poor light.   There is, of course, the possibility that
Limpy was the finger man in the case; the attorneys
are working on that assumption.

We scoured the city and, later, all parts of the
country for Limpy.   The paper even offered a reward
for information leading to his whereabouts, but he has
disappeared.

By the time the principals in the graft case were
brought into court for a hearing on their indictments,
I was a prisoner out on bond, and my word wasn't
worth a cent.   Hanley, the district attorney, seemed
especially lackadaisical in his efforts to prosecute the
cases, and the judge threw them out of court.   Then
Hanley gave a statement to the other papers contend-
ing that his office had been made the victim of a
gigantic hoax story, and promising to prosecute me to
the limit of the law.   As a result, the aldermen and
the car dealer filed suits for false arrest, defamation
of character and malicious slander against the *Record*
for over a million dollars.   The law suits are now
pending; should the paper lose them and be forced to
pay damages, it may mean the closing of the doors.

My trial lasted only three days, for we had little to
offer by way of evidence.   I was found guilty on the
first ballot.   The judge denied my appeal for a new
trial, and the powerful political machine I'd sought to
buck had me safely in Stony Point less than two
months after the frame-up was staged.   Now Hanley
is running for governor.   If he's elected, I'm afraid
I'm sunk.

Three months ago, they handcuffed me and took me to Stony Point. I said good-by to Joyce and the boys from the paper in the county jail.

"We'll never stop working on your case for a minute, Frank," said Joyce.

Joe Campbell, Bill Mason and Lew Keller muttered that they'd have me out in no time, with a lot of city officials and an automobile dealer to take my place in prison.

I held Joyce's hands, the cuffs rattling as I drew her close to me. I felt pretty low. There wasn't much I could say—didn't dare risk trying to say much, anyway. My throat was too choked.

"Write often," she said. "I'll just die if I don't hear from you."

"I will. I'll write every time I can. And you kind of watch out for my mother."

"We'll get you out. They can't keep an innocent man in prison." There were tears in her eyes.

But three months have slowly slipped away, and with the passage of each day I lose a little more of my hope. I know that Joyce is raising heaven and earth to help me—that Bill and Lew and Joe and everybody else on the paper are doing everything they can in my behalf—but I'm beginning to fear that if anything is going to turn up, it would have done so by now. The time is getting long.

The first month I was here, I applied for a pardon. The petition was denied on the ground that the evidence offered in court justified my conviction. Now I can't apply for a pardon again for a year and a half, for such are the rules governing the pardon board. About the only hope I have of going home before the parole board hears my application next December is that some evidence will be unearthed in the meantime which will insure my being granted a new trial. And I'm not so sure I'd care to accept a parole. It might look like an admission of guilt. Then, too, from gossip I've heard here in Stony Point, the parole board won't let paroled inmates work for newspapers.

The past compares itself with the present—with Mueller, an old-time safe-blower, who is serving life imprisonment under the habitual criminal act; with Lassiter, a former cashier in a small upstate bank, who accepted several deposits after being aware of the bank's insolvency, and who received a ten-year sentence on a legal technicality; with Stacey and Garsky and two of the prison's rats. . . . The past compares itself with the high gray walls, the shops, the cell halls, the great barred windows which rise the height of the buildings themselves, and the uniformed guards who pace the catwalks on top of the walls, guns at the alert, and those who stalk omnipotently among thirty-five hundred gray-clad convicts.

3

WE SLUMP down on the grass, our backs toward the warm bricks of the north cell hall.

Mueller says, "Ross, now you see what I'm getting at. It wasn't bad enough to get the book on a bum rap. I got to do the time in this stir among rats like Ludke and Carlisle."

Mueller's plight is constantly on his mind. He swears to his innocence at every opportunity; as a consequence, he is losing control and daily comes a little closer to the borderline of insanity. Lassiter and I try to help him, but in prison there isn't much we can do.

"Don't let it get you down again, Mueller," cautions Lassiter softly. "Do your time as easy as you can. Keep your mind off yourself, like the rest of the fellows."

"It's different with the guys that're guilty," cries Mueller. "They pulled their capers and knew what they'd get if they were caught. But me—there I was, minding my own business and keeping my nose clean— going straight for the first time in twenty years, by God, when those dirty cops put the bite on me and got me the book on a bum rap. I've lived forty-four years, but if it was in the cards that I absolutely had to take a fall on a bum rap, could I get just one little break in all my life and do this time in a decent stir like Stillwater or Sing Sing? Hell, no! My luck couldn't stand it. I had to fall in this lousy state."

Because the prison, its rules and its officers are much closer to him and more a part of his life, Mueller does not vent his spleen on the judge and court which he says unjustly imprisoned him, but on his immediate surroundings. The silent system especially gripes him, as it does most of the other inmates. Talking is permitted only during twenty minutes of the noon meal and on special occasions such as Saturday afternoons while we're in the yard, and on holidays. Infractions of the talking rules mean the immediate loss of all privileges for a week, or, in some instances, solitary confinement—"the hole."

"Just take it easy and mark time till the pardon board springs you," counsels the gentle Lassiter. "Make off you're doing this time for something you pulled but never got picked up on."

"Not that I haven't pulled plenty that was never hung on me," says Mueller. "I have, but not in this state. I don't owe this state anything. I was driving truck and going straight. My record convicted me."

"It might be worse though," says Lassiter. "Suppose you'd got scared and started to run and the cops had killed you instead of taking you in? This way you've got a chance to get out and start all over again some day."

"Killed! By God, I'd rather be dead than doing time in here. I tell you it's a madhouse—work like hell all

day, then sit in your cell until next morning with nothing to do but stare at the wall. And not so much as
a picture clipping from a magazine or newspaper
allowed on the wall. Screws snooping past your cell
every few minutes, trying to catch you at something so
they can have you thrown in the hole. First thing you
know, you're stir nuts and just mark time till you can
get out and kill the first son-of-a-bitch that crosses
your path. No wonder there's so much insanity and
suicide in here. . . . Sometimes I think I'm going nuts
myself. I catch myself mumbling under my breath.
I look in the mirror and cuss the warden and the deputies and the screws . . ." Mueller blinks and stares at
his feet. "I wonder," he adds, "if the joint's getting
me."

"Don't worry," chuckles Lassiter, "there isn't a guy
who's been here six months that doesn't have the same
symptoms." But he flashes me a troubled glance. And
then, to Mueller, "Anyway, what's the diff? We'll
both be out of here when the pardon board meets again
next fall."

Lassiter has applied for a commutation of sentence;
and Mueller, who was found guilty of burglary, hopes
to secure a full pardon. But during the three months
I've been here, I've learned that the pardon board of
this state relies almost entirely upon the decision of the
judge and the jury, and is governed, in most cases, ac-
cordingly. My own case is an indication of this.

There's some hope for Lassiter. This is his first
slip; he has more than a little outside influence and some

support politically, which latter means a great deal in Stony Point. His sentence may be commuted by the pardon board. But Mueller, who is both broke and friendless, hasn't much chance. In spite of his steadfast plea of innocence, his past record may keep him here for a good many years to come. Yet, though the jury refused to believe him and the pardon board probably will do likewise, we feel that he is innocent. And this is a strange condition, for the prison is full of "innocent" men who scream to high heaven of the injustice that is being heaped upon them—this despite their confessions to their crimes and pleas of guilty without even going to trial! We all laugh at their absurd stories—the stories which they expect the pardon board to believe. . . . But Mueller doesn't even try to bolster up his sagging hopes by telling himself that his plea may be granted. He knows, and doesn't try to kid himself out of it, that his case is nearly hopeless.

But I say, "What the hell, Mueller. Even if they turn you down, you've got in over three years. And I've heard of many lifers who killed somebody and came in and went out in less time than that."

"Yeah," mutters Mueller. "Guys with dough and plenty of outside connections. Oh, I'll go out, all right—in a hearse, out the back gate." He gazes silently at the poplar trees, whose crowns, a mist of green, rise above the north wall. "I'm going nuts, I guess," he adds, "just thinking about it. Life! And in this madhouse!"

Lassiter wrinkles his brow and eyes me obliquely.

"Take it easy," he counsels Mueller. "Don't let the joint get you. You've done time in too many of these places to let this one bother you."

"That's easy enough for you to say," snorts Mueller, "when you're talking about somebody else's time. And you've never been in any other stir than this; you think they're all alike. But they aren't. They treat you like men in all the other stirs I've been in. But here they've got a set of rules that were made for kids, and they treat you like dogs on top of it. . . . Kick you around. Beat you with canes. Handcuff you to the bars all day. Make you go all winter without even a minute for exercise. Can't talk. Can't smile. Can't make a motion with your hands. Can't even pick something off the floor of the shop without raising your hand and getting permission to bend over. And nothing to eat but beans, beans, beans. . . . When I think I'm doing this time for nothing, is it any wonder I'm blowing my top?"

"I don't mean to stick up for the joint," says Lassiter, "and I admit it's tough as hell to do time here, but they do pay us a little so we can buy soap and tobacco and can have a few bucks saved for when we go out. . . . Thirty-five cents a day isn't much, but we'd be a lot more miserable if they didn't pay us anything. . . . If you'll kind of try to remember that, bad as it is, it could be even worse, maybe you'll feel a little better."

"Worse," snaps Mueller. "It couldn't be any worse. The money don't make any difference. This is the toughest stir in the United States. And I ought to know. I've been in plenty of them. And my friends have told me about the others. . . . Alcatraz! I get a laugh out of the guff the newspapers put out about that joint. Why the hell don't those reporters come down here and see a stir that's really tough? . . . Every time you bat an eye in here, they take away your privileges. Look at that time I was in the hospital with pneumonia. That dirty croaker and his rat head nurse had me tossed in the hole, sick as I was, just because I put up a howl for not getting any treatment. And the warden didn't give a damn. Wouldn't even listen to me when I was in the hole burning up with a fever. They figure it's okay to dump a guy in a cot and let him either die or get well, if he don't take too long about doing it. And if he hollers, throw him in the hole and let him rot. . . . And these screws—they're a pack of the dirtiest mongrels I've ever seen. Especially Pete. What a time I'd have killing that pot-bellied little rat!"

Pete Kassock, our shop guard, may be small but he more than offsets his size with his malevolence. He is a ridiculous-appearing little man—short and bald and shaped like an egg—but he makes our lives a continuous hell. Some of the lifers and long-timers would kill him were it not, paradoxically, for the fact that capital punishment has long been outlawed in this state, and murder by a prisoner is punishable by life in soli-

tary confinement—"the book in the hole." A big
Negro, who was already doing life, smashed a former deputy's skull with an iron pipe. The deputy
died. The Negro was taken down to the county seat
for trial, got life all over again, and has been in the
hole ever since. That was twelve years ago. . . .
Many a lifer or long-timer would welcome the chair or
hanging if he could exchange his life for Pete's. But
life in the hole is a long, long time.

When Pete dislikes an inmate—and he instinctively
dislikes anyone who displays the slightest amount of
intelligence—he purposely rides the man until he can
stand no more and blows up, telling Pete what he
thinks of him, answering insolently, or otherwise committing some other infraction of the rules. Then Pete
"reports" the inmate—"sends him to court," as it is
known—and the hole receives a new tenant. After that
the inmate must wait at least nine more months before
he is again eligible for parole and forfeits all privileges
for thirty days or more.

Through Pete's efforts, Fargo Red, who works with
Stacey and me in Pete's shop, has served more than
seven years of a twenty-year sentence and has never
yet been interviewed by the parole board, though he
should have been eligible for parole after serving ten
months. But each time Red was about to be called
before the board, Pete had him thrown into the hole—
once for leaving a half-cooked piece of sow-belly un-
eaten on his plate, once for passing a "permitted"
magazine to another inmate in the cell hall—all "ex-

changes" are supposed to be handled by the mail
clerks—and innumerable times for equally trivial infractions of the rules. . . . Of course Red should
watch his step and not do the things that get him into
trouble, but he's just a big dumb ox and continually
gets into harmless mischief.

"Pete's a tough nut to crack, all right," says Lassiter,
which is about as close as he ever comes to condemn-
ing anyone or anything. "Swell guy to work for."
He chuckles. "Did you hear him yesterday noon
when I asked for a pair of clean pants? Boy, I
thought he'd bust a vein!"

Mueller spits disgustedly. " 'Why d'yuh wanna
change them pants?'-" he whines, simulating Pete's
peculiarly squeaky voice. " 'God damn you, y' jist
got clean pants six weeks ago. Y' sleep in the alleys
on the outside, an' when y' git in jail you're hollerin'
fer clean pants!' "

"Just a pal," grins Lassiter, who is one of the tidiest
men in the institution.

Mueller curses obscenely and adds, "I'd like to see
him try that stuff in Columbus or Dannemora. Those
guys'd cut his heart right out and make him eat it . . ."
He stares unseeingly at the grass. And then, "He'd
better lay off riding you. I'm about fed up. I can
take everything he dishes out, but damned if I'll stand
by and see him ride a pal of mine into the nut house"—
the constant fear of every inmate.

Lassiter slaps Mueller's arm.

"Don't worry about me, kid. Pete doesn't bother
me at all."

Mueller opens his mouth to reply, but a shadow falls across us. We look up. . . . There are the dirty, baggy blue uniform trousers, the worn, shiny coat, the egg-like form and the little pig eyes of Pete.

"Git up outta that dirt!" he howls. "Where th' hell d'yuh think y'are—in some county jail? Lassiter—lookit yuh, wallerin' around like a hog in a mudhole! Git up an' stand at attention when a officer speaks t' yuh!"

We scramble to our feet and shuffle uneasily in front of him. He glowers hotly at us, puffing audibly.

"I didn't know it was against the rules to sit on the grass," says Lassiter. "A lot of the other men are doing it."

"Shut your trap! One more crack outta you an' I'll have y' in th' hole. If they's any talkin' t' be done around here, I'm th' guy that'll do it. . . . Lookit yuh, the whole pack of yuh—how long y' gotta be around here b'fore y'll know enough t' salute an' fold your arms when a officer speaks t' yuh?"

We stand silently, but he senses our quiet rebellion.

"Salute!" he screams, pounding the grass with his lead-tipped cane—the central part of every officer's equipment. "Every one of yuh—salute!"

Mechanically we salute, then stand shoulder to shoulder with folded arms. The inmates near by cease their aimless milling about. Their faces are grim as they watch Pete. They suffer with us in our humiliation. But the guards quickly break up the watchers and start them moving again. And as the mass of gray-clad men parts, and slowly shuffles away, I see Ludke and Carlisle laughing over our disgrace and radiating their approval of Pete's tactics.

Pete catches my line of observation and swings around. When he sees the pair, he shows his yellow teeth in a grin of encouragement. . . . I steal a glance at Mueller. His face is dead white. His lips twitch. His gaze is centered on the tops of the poplar trees beyond the north wall.

Pete's attention returns to us. "Buncha ignorant tin-horn thieves!" he snorts. "Never knowed nothing, never will, and when you git in here, y' try t' outsmart somebody that knows more'n the whole of yuh put together." He waddles away, muttering to Ludke and Carlisle, who join him fawningly, "Show them tramps who's boss around here."

Mac, the night screw on our gallery, passes us. He's a swell guy and always willing to go out of his way to make our lot a little easier. . . . He winks surreptitiously, then raises his eyebrows in the direction Pete and the rats have taken.

"Who's your friend?" he jibes. And passes on.

Our tension eases. Lassiter screws up his face. "Yes sir," he drawls, "Pete's certainly one nice guy. Hope I meet him on the outside sometime."

"I'll meet him," snarls Mueller. "And maybe I won't wait till I'm on the outside. He's gonna ride us just once too often, and then he's liable to wake up in the morgue. . . . I got nothing to lose by bumping him. I'm doing the book anyway."

Lassiter looks serious. "Listen, Mueller," he cautions, "if you've really got any idea like that in your head, forget it. If you killed Pete, they'd take you down to the county seat and give you the book for murder and bury you in that hole for the rest of your life. And don't think you'd be doing the rest of us a favor by bumping Pete. There'd be somebody just as bad or worse to take his place, and they'd make the rules even tighter than they are now."

"I'd sooner be doing the book in the hole than working any longer for Pete. The deputy won't transfer me to another shop, so I've got to get out of there some other way. . . . Besides, I might have a chance to escape from the courtroom."

"That's sure death," I point out. "Every guy that ever tried to beat it from the courtrooms was either killed or captured on the spot."

"Yes," adds Lassiter, "and there was a guy that thought he could make it out of the window. He splashed all over the concrete driveway below. . . . Just take it easy for a few months and we'll get a break when the pardon board meets."

"Break!" cries Mueller. "The only break I'll get is when I go out that back gate in a box. . . . You guys think I'm scared of dying? Hell! If I was sure of dying for it, I'd rip Pete's guts out with a bale hook in a minute."

Lassiter eyes me apprehensively. When Mueller broods overly on Pete he is a raging maniac and we are hard put to keep him out of trouble. Only the pos-

sibility that the pardon board may, after all, give him
some kind of break keeps him from blowing up now.
And during the months which lie ahead, Lassiter and
I are going to have a tough job keeping Mueller's
homicidal fires under control. After that, if the pardon
board turns him down——

"Wait till we get out," urges Lassiter. "We'll meet
Pete some day. We're bound to. And then we'll see
what happens."

"Boy," I say, "what I wouldn't like to do to him
with a blacksnake whip."

"Whip!" snorts Mueller. "Talking about whips
when you could just as well be thinking you were
pounding nails in his belly, or something like that."

"A man can get a lot of satisfaction out of a blacksnake whip," observes Lassiter mildly. "Once I saw
a planter in Florida working on a colored boy with
one."

"You can't get the kind of satisfaction I want,"
growls Mueller. "And if that's the best you can think
of, your ideas aren't so hot either."

"Oh, I'm not a very violent man," admits Lassiter,
"and I'm easily satisfied. But I could think up a thing
or two if I had the mind. For instance, how'd it be to
tie Pete up naked on a plank, and cook him with a
steam hose till his fat hide was so tender you could
stick your fingers through it? Then how'd it be to
smear him with honey and stake him out on an ant hill
and watch the ants eat him alive?"

"Lousy!" snorts Mueller.

"Lousy?" I cry. "I think it's swell!"

Lassiter grins. "Well, then, we'll let the old tor-turer himself tell us how it should be done. . . . Come on, Mueller—tell us poor ignorant souls the proper way to torture a man."

Mueller stares at his shoes. His lips twitch. His eyes burn. But Lassiter doesn't realize Mueller's con-dition.

"Come on," kids Lassiter, nudging Mueller. "Don't hold out on us."

Mueller slams his fist into his palm. "You want to know what I'd do?" he cries. His eyes narrow, his lips tighten, and words start crackling from his mouth. "Why, God damn him, I'd hold matches against his bare feet and cook his toes off one by one. I'd burn off his fingers and his ears and his nose. I'd take a hammer and knock all his teeth out. I'd break his arms and legs into a million pieces. I'd tear his eyes out with red-hot pliers. I'd cook those fat cheeks of his and let the dogs chew the meat right down to the bone. I'd slit open his pot-belly and rip his guts out with my bare hands, and tramp on them with hob-nailed boots. I'd ——" He chokes. His eyes are two burning embers in an alabaster cast. His hatred is alive, terrible, a thing that consumes him. . . . Lassiter turns to me in alarm and shakes his head. Mueller leans against the cell hall and shuts his eyes. "Just the sight of him suffering," he mutters weakly. "Jesus!"

My flesh crawls.

4

LASSITER spies a roving inmate and cries, "Oh, oh! Here he comes. Fargo Red."

It is the hairy man whom Pete has kept here for over seven years—so-called not because of his hair, which is black and shaggy, but in honor of his flaming crimson nose, "paid fer," as he puts it, "with good alcohol at a buck a pint." He is huge and noisy, walks with the shambling gait of an ape, and is addicted to great quantities of chewing tobacco, homemade snuff and profanity. To Red, a day is never merely fine or nice. Such adjectives are entirely too colorless. So the day becomes either "God-damn swell" or "God-damn lousy"; and his best friend is a "swell old son-of-a-bitch," but in a different tone from his enemy, who is a "no-good rat bastard" or something equally light. Red's proudest boasts are that the brakeman never lived who could throw him out of a boxcar, that he has done time in practically every jail in America, and that he was once the official dog-catcher of Fargo, North Dakota—his home town—but was "removed from office" because he "didn't have the heart t' kill them poor purps, an' turned 'em loose as fast as they was ketched." Red is our comic relief, an ageless person who makes us laugh when it's easier to cry.

His questing eye sights us and he storms across the grass.

41

"So here y' are. I been scoutin' the whole joint fer yuh."

He glares at us as though we are at the bottom of all his troubles.

"What's up, Red?" I ask. "Borrowing tobacco to pay your bets again?"

"Hell, no." He spits a brown stream, and his palm removes the spray from his chin. "I'm collectin' to-day, fer a change. But you guys gotta settle a argu-ment fer me first. . . . See that guy over there?" He indicates a sad-eyed little inmate who sits discon-solately on his haunches and searches his teeth with a splinter. "Whaddya think he had the guts t' try an' hand me? Says whales've got teats an' give milk, same's a cow!"

Lassiter roars. "Now it's whales!" Red is forever running up to us to settle some crackpot bet he's made.

"Ain't that the pay-off?" grins Red. "Well, first thing I knows he wants t' bet. So we bets a couple cans of tobacco. Then he thinks it over an' can't re-member where he seen it or heard it—some book or some guy or something—so he wants t' call the bet off. 'Nothing doing,' I says, an' starts right out t' find you guys an' prove it."

Lassiter and I howl. Even Mueller grins feebly.

Red mutters, "What's so funny about that?"

Lassiter says, "Go and pay him the two cans of tobacco."

"What!"

"Whales aren't fish, you big skull." He slaps Red

a terrific clout on the shoulder. "They're mammals
and give milk just like any other animal. What do
you suppose they come to the surface and blow for?
They can't live under water for any length of time.
They'd drown."

"Well, I'll be a low-born snide! Are you nuts, too?"

I say, "That's right, Red. Take a look in the dic-
tionary."

Red snorts, "I don't believe a word of it."

Nevertheless he rushes off in the direction of the
sad-eyed little man, talks earnestly for a moment, waves
his arms violently, winds up as though he is about to
clout the little man on the head, then charges back.

Lassiter says, "Did you pay him, Red?"

"Hell, no! You think I'm nuts like you guys? I
let him call the bet off like he wanted to in the first
place."

"Just too big-hearted for your own good, hey, Red?"

"Yeah. That's me all over—big, bad Red, the
friend of the working man. I got soft in the head and
let him talk me outta the bet. But he's bum pay, and
I figgered I'd save a fight and a trip to the hole by
letting him call it off. He wouldn't of paid me anyway, and I'd of had to lick him fer the tobacco." He
frowns as though he is trying to corner a forgotten
thought. "Whales give milk! Now whaddya know
about that!"

Lassiter howls and pounds my shoulder. Red grins
sheepishly. "I still think you guys was ribbing me."

"What's the little guy in here for, Red?" I ask.

"Who, Suggs? Oh, him! What a dope! He's a boxcar thief. He stole a hundred-pound sack of walnuts and hid them in the ground. Then he got caught on some other deal and they give him two years. Now he sits around and worries fer fear the squirrels'll find the nuts before he gits out."

Another burst of laughter is immediately stifled when Pete pushes through a group of inmates and halts before us. He looks us over slowly, a frown closing his little pig eyes to narrow slits. The look he directs at Red is murderous. Their warfare is open and perpetual—a thing that started raging the first day Red entered Pete's shop, and which Red has kept burning ever since. . . . Pete growls something about bums and waddles away.

"There he goes," snarls Red—"the dirtiest, rottenest, no-good son-of-a-bitch in America! He'd beat his own mother. He'd laugh at a strangling baby. He'd——" Red sputters impotently.

We saunter across the yard toward the sidelines. Red eyes the water fountain.

"What're Stacey and Garsky doing over there?" he demands.

Mueller tells the story of Stacey and the rats who snitched on him.

"Them dirty lice," growls Red. "Now a good guy's gotta go to the hole, while people like them can run all over the joint. . . . Where they at now?"

"Don't go stirring up any trouble, Red," cautions Lassiter. "You've been in that hole enough. It'll be too bad if you get into another battle."

"Well, they don't wanna show their faces around me."

At this moment, Carlisle and Ludke emerge from the sidelines and start across the prison yard in our direction. Red is off to meet them.

Lassiter calls, "Come back here, Red"; but when the hairy man doesn't heed him, Lassiter says to us, "Let's go. He'll take them both on if we don't stop him; then he'll be in the hole as well as Stacey."

We overtake Red as he confronts the two rats. He minces no words.

"You two dirty rat sons-a-bitches! So y' been snitching again!"

"What's eating you?" asks Ludke.

Red pushes against them threateningly. "You know damn well what's eating me. You've snitched on Ross and me, and now you snitched on Stacey. You're gonna make that hole with a pair of busted jaws fer company."

The two rats give ground and start looking wildly for an officer. Mac, the friendly night screw, hurries over, takes Red by the arm, and pulls him away.

"Break it up," Mac orders. "You out of your mind, Red? They'll bury you in the hole for starting a fight out here where it might spread."

Ludke and Carlisle now seek to press their claim.

"He tried to start a battle with us," they chorus. "We weren't doing a thing, and he threatened to kill us."

Mac, who has continued to lead the hairy man away, now must pause and heed the complaint of Carlisle and Ludke. Mac turns to us.

"That the truth?" he asks. "How about it, Ross? Did you see Red try to start a fight or hear him make any threats?"

"No," I lie, wishing I could say worse. "Red didn't do or say a thing. We were walking along minding our own business when these two rats came running across the yard at us. They were the ones who tried to start a fight so we'd get thrown in the hole."

Mueller growls, "That's right," and spits on the ground, narrowly missing the feet of Carlisle.

The rats start howling with murderous glances at me. "Ross's lying. He's had it in for us ever since we came here."

Mac pretends to be raising his cane. "Go on, beat it," he cries at the rats. "In about a minute, I'll have you both in the hole for lying and trying to start a fight."

Carlisle snarls at me, "You'll be sorry for this."

Mac says, "Are you going to start moving or will I take you in?"

The rats now ignore Red and center their hate on me.

"You've stuck your neck out, wise guy," sneers Carlisle. "Now you'll get it chopped off."

They flee toward the north cell hall, where they stop and talk excitedly and occasionally point at us.

Mac says, "Watch your step. I may get in trouble for having sided with you; so if they tell the deputy, just stick to your stories and I'll stick to mine."

"I don't think they'll get very far with that kind of a snitch to the deputy warden," says Lassiter. "He hates the guts of a rat."

"Yes," agrees Mac, "but he's got to listen or something might get past that would lead to something else big. . . . You'd better watch out now, Ross," he continues. "They'll be out to get you. I can warn you if they report you to me—they stop me nearly every night on my rounds and snitch on somebody. But it won't be so simple if they frame you on something and report it to another guard. . . . You see, the hell of it is, we've got to turn in a report to the deputy when they snitch for fear they'll follow up their tale and snitch to him too. Then we'd be in dutch for not making a report in the first place."

"You gonna report this now?" asks Red.

"No. I'll take a chance. But watch your step."

We move away.

"What a guy!" says Lassiter.

"Almost be a pleasure to do time here if all the screws were like Mac," observes Red.

Mueller warns me, "You'll have to watch those rats now. They're poison."

"Yeah," adds Red. "They was sore enough that time you dropped a bale on Carlisle."

"What was that?" asks Lassiter.

"They snitched on Ross and me fer talking when they first come here, and we both got sent to court. Ross was up on top the manila pile, lowering a bale a couple days afterwards, and Carlisle was at the bottom, looking up and giving Ross the laugh. Bale slipped out and fell on the rat. Ever since, he's swore Ross did it on purpose, because he got sent to court."

"They acted like they hate your guts plenty now," says Mueller. "They forgot all about Red starting the argument."

"Sore because I lied and got them in bad with Mac," I say. "But I don't care. They've got that and plenty more coming to them."

"They'll get it too if they don't lay off," promises Red. "But now that they've really lined up against you, watch out. They're like a couple of snakes."

We reach the sidelines and watch the game. Most of the inmates are booing the prison team and betting tobacco and fountain pens—the common denominator of prison trade—as soon as an officer's back is turned.

Mueller fixes his eye on the north cell hall.

"Well," he mutters angrily, "I see they found the soda."

Deputy Armstrong and Temple, the captain of the solitary cell hall, are descending the stone steps. They peer about the yard, then head for the drinking fountain. An inmate—I see it is Garsky—sidles hurriedly toward the baseball diamond. Stacey waits defiantly for the deputy and the captain to seize his arms and march him off to the hole.

5

RED shuts off the twine machine—we have been operating it alone since Stacey went to the hole last month—and holds up his hand for permission to leave his position. After what seems an eternity of waiting, Pete nods his head and Red starts for the latrine. Behind the clothes rack, which juts out into the shop and hides the latrine and the mop room from Pete, I can see Mose, the Negro swamper who cleans up around the shop. And then I know why Red left the machine so determinedly. For Mose is our information bureau. Besides mopping the floor, cleaning Pete's spittoon, shining Pete's shoes and doing other menial tasks, Mose also has access to Pete's files and can give out the dope concerning any inmate who works in this shop. And Red has probably got some question to put to Mose.

I can see Red talking with Mose—a process which entails Red's stooping down in the latrine and speaking beneath the half-partition which separates the toilet from the mop room. It's the only safe way that we can speak with the porter, for he's not allowed back by our machine, and Pete's hawk-like eye misses nothing that's done in the open. His pencil is always ready to write out a report that will cost us a week's privileges.

Red returns; then when Pete's face is pointed the other way, Red pulls me down behind the twine machine where we won't be seen talking.

"Mose just told me Stacey's been in D. W."—the detention ward—"but's due out today."

"Good," I say. "How much time did he do in the hole?"

"Nine days. Then he got smart and said he wouldn't go back to work for Pete while he was still in third grade, so the deputy let him do the other twenty-one days in D.W. where Pete couldn't give him any bum reports and keep him from getting out of third grade."

Red lines his jaws with homemade snuff, then spits pensively on the floor and rubs it in with his foot. I rise cautiously and peer over the top of the machine. Pete occasionally slips up on us when we are out of sight—as we must be when we stop the machine to clean out the debris and ends of fiber which would otherwise cause a breakdown. . . . Until recently Pete always sent the crew that worked this machine to court every time they were out of sight; but an inmate who worked here until just before I was assigned to this shop wrote the state board of control in complaint, and Pete got orders to lay off writing reports on this crew if the machine was shut down for cleaning or repairs and he saw none of the crew talking. . . . Thus we take advantage of the opportunity to talk, even though Pete in his rage swore that the first man he caught talking would be thrown in the hole. But we must talk. The continued silence has driven too many inmates insane. . . . Before Stacey went to the hole, one of us stood guard while the other two talked. Now, until Stacey returns, Red and I must take our chances.

"I'm getting fed up," complains Red. "Working in this shop's like being one of the animals in the zoo."

"Well, Pete's a nice keeper, anyway, Red."

The hairy man curses. "They got a lotta guts letting that louse run a shop. We may be bad guys, but we ain't so bad we deserve that kinda treatment."

"You ought to get one of the *Record's* sob sisters to help you."

"Sob sisters! They ain't never yet helped anybody that deserved it. They get guys like Carlisle and Ludke out and leave fellows like us in. . . . Sob sisters! A lot they know about cons and prisons. All they care about is getting some louse out that belongs in for life. You watch; they'll probably be trying to spring Carlisle and Ludke. And God knows they're the dirtiest lice in the joint. . . . It's just like I've always said. These joints ain't so bad. It's the ringtails you gotta do the time with." His lips purse and a brown sea slaps the floor. "Carlisle and the Wolf and Ludke and Cooper and about fifty others. And the worst of it is, not a one of them kind of people draws as much as a ten spot, and I get twenty years fer stealing a tire. Justice! They call that justice. Some owly-eyed old bastard of a judge don't like your looks, or mebbe he was on a drunk the night before, so he glares at you and decides, 'Now, there's a no-good son-of-a-bitch'; and before you can say boo, he's yelling, 'Twenty years—take him away!' You can pull pretty near every kind of a dirty caper in this state and get away with it, but God help your fanny if you git drunk and bust into a garage and steal a used tire. . . . I wish t' Christ I'd stayed home with my old lady in Fargo."

His tirade is halted when the inmate at the rear of the machine rings the bell for Red or me to start it up. The machine, known as the "breaker," because it breaks up the raw fiber, is about forty feet long and resembles the structural work of a railway coal gondola. An inmate known as the "feeder" spreads the raw manila and sisal on the endless belt at the rear of the machine. At the turn of the belt, a series of heavy double-rollers receives the material and compresses it, passing it on to the first of two endless chains. These chains are studded with long sharp spikes. The first of the chains is slow-moving and carries the material through a bath of oil which is sprayed down from above. In the oil is a poison which kills any bugs that try to eat the twine, once it is in the field and used for bundling grain. . . . At the turn of the first chain, a second, which moves very fast, takes the ends of the fibers and combs them out, the first chain holding the main load of fiber so that it is thoroughly combed before it is released. Then the material pours from the spout of the machine in an endless skein. The operator must pound this skein into a three-sided box at the front of the machine until he has formed a three-hundred-pound bale. As fast as the bales are completed, another inmate drags them from the box and weighs them. After the operator has piled ten bales—"one set"—he is relieved by the inmate who weighed the bales, and the pair change places. . . . I have seen men faint at this task—big men who looked strong. It is at such work that Stacey, Red and I serve our time.

Red is just completing his set and I am filling the oil tank with the solution that is sprayed on the twine fiber when an inmate wearing the second grade uniform enters the shop. I think at first that he is another new man, but after he has donned overalls and headed for the breaker I see it is Stacey—hair shaved off, just out of third grade.

According to the prison regulations, an inmate is in third grade until thirty days after going to the hole. After his release from solitary, and during his period in third grade, he receives no privileges at all. His hair is shaved off on the day he leaves the hole, and he cannot smoke, chew, read, write, receive mail, visitors or pay, and is allowed no recreation. On Saturday afternoons, when the rest of the prisoners have three hours' liberty in the yard, the third-grader is locked in his cell. During the noon meal, the only time, except yard time, when talking is permitted, the third-grader sits at a special table and maintains a rigid silence. And he must go thirty consecutive days without a demerit mark before he can become a second-grade prisoner. Some of the officers, especially Pete, seem to take a particular delight in letting a third-grader go for twenty-nine days without a mark, and then reporting him for some minor infraction of the rules, in which event the prisoner has the whole thing to do over again. . . . Second-grade prisoners are ineligible for parole and may write only twice a month. Aside from this, they receive the same privileges as the first-graders. Some inmates have been kept in third grade as long as eleven months; others have got out of third grade in the minimum of thirty days but have remained in second grade for years, the same rule of thirty consecutive days without a mark applying to second-graders who have been in the hole. Many men have spent their entire sentences in second and third grade, never being interviewed by the parole board. . . . If an officer dislikes an inmate, the unhappy fellow may have to do his entire sentence as a consequence, for in this state the courts operate under the indeterminate sentence law. Neither the warden—a more or less legendary figure who is seldom seen—nor the deputy warden takes an inmate's word for anything, which is probably just as well and rather to be expected.

Pete is keeping an eye on Stacey, so I remain where I am, behind the oil tank. Red is busy at the front end of the machine, piling his set, so he doesn't see Stacey duck from sight the minute Pete's back is turned and scuttle crab-like on all fours across the floor to a stack of spare parts that are ranged along the back wall. The breaker hides Stacey from Pete, who is up on his raised platform yelling something at the foreman, and a pile of raw twine fiber conceals Stacey from the rest of the inmates. Except me. Standing there, waiting for the tank to fill, I see him dig into a heap of extra gears and pulleys and spiked crossbars and bring up the wickedest looking knife I've seen in a long time. He evidently made it from a file and hid it there before he went to the hole. . . . The knife is seven or eight inches long.

Stacey takes the tip of the blade between his right thumb and forefinger and lets fly at a bale of sisal. The knife sinks in to the hilt. The sisal is packed under hydraulic pressure before it is sent to the prison, so Stacey has to tug pretty hard to get the knife out. He repeats the feat six or eight times. Then I notice that he's throwing the knife with his eyes closed. So accurate is he that from a distance of ten or fifteen feet, blind, the knife sticks in almost the same spot each time. . . . Then I recall his former knife-throwing proclivities before he turned bank robber. But I figure it's a screwy thing to be pulling now, for if Pete gets off the platform and catches Stacey with the knife, he won't get out of the hole till he's walking on his beard. And then I remember Ludke and Carlisle, the rats who sent Stacey to the hole, and I feel a slight chill.

Stacey suddenly tucks the knife beneath his shirt and, as though he senses someone else, glances up quickly. I smile confusedly and make off I'm clapping my hands. His face is a human skull thinly veiled with yellow tissue. I beckon that Pete may see him. He laughs, crouching there on all fours, and crawls back to the breaker. I shut off the oil and kneel beside him.

"How'd they handle you?" I shout above the roar of the machinery—small danger of Pete's hearing us and sending us to court: ten machines are running and the shop is noisier than a boiler factory.

"Can't kick."

"Need anything—soap, tobacco, toothpaste?"

"No. They gave me my stuff when I shed my stripes."

My stomach is hollow from the sight of that flying shiv and the look on Stacey's face. He keeps searching my eyes, as if he is looking for something that will warn him of danger. . . . Words are hard for me to find.

"Well," I say, "let me know if you need anything. And watch out for Pete. He's owlier than usual today."

I start to rise, but Stacey's hand catches me.

"Listen, Frank. Forget about that shiv."

I feign bewilderment—I haven't been around here for four months without learning at least some of the answers.

"What shiv?" I ask, smiling. "Never heard the word before."

"This shiv." He pulls the knife from under his shirt and holds it close to my nose.

I hold my smile. "I still don't see any."

Then some of the tension leaves his face and he puts the knife away. But his eyes are two bits of bright ice in an impassible mask. He slaps my arm.

"Okay, Ross."

As I enter my cell that night after supper, the letter for which I watch each day is lying on the cot. From Joyce. Somehow, each evening when I find a message from her, the first picture that comes to my mind is the one I always saw when I entered the newspaper office: Joyce's dark head above a typewriter—her fingers flying on some story which she was getting ready for the next edition—a stack of clippings piled beside her machine—her coat hung loosely over the back of her chair. And then there was always the smile that flashed when I walked silently to her and placed my hands on her shoulders. It was a special smile, I always liked to think—a special smile only for me that seemed to say we had some big secret which we were keeping just for ourselves. And there was always something that went beyond beauty in her smile—something in the way her lips curled just a little bit at the corners, and her nose wrinkled, and her white teeth flashed, and her eyes first sparkled, then became very tender. And there was the unconscious little motion she made toward her hair. It seemed that one or two tresses were always hanging just a bit awry and she must pat them back while she smiled and spoke. . . . That is the picture I see every time I find the envelope with the *Mountain Record's* return address and Joyce's neat typing lying on my cot.

Her letter brings good news:

My darling,
    At last I can come to see you. I've just returned from a visit with the Governor, and he has

given permission for me to come down to the prison once a month, even though I'm not a relative. He decided that inasmuch as we'll be married as soon as you're free, I'm practically related to you now. Isn't that fine? It's nearly killed me, not being able to see you during these four long months.

Your mother is feeling well and wants to visit you, but I've kept her from coming down to the prison so far. Can't you forget your not wanting her to see you in there? She's old, I know, and it would hurt her to remember you as you now are, but I think it hurts her still more not to see you at all. After all, she's your mother, and the sight of you in a prison uniform would be better than not seeing you at all. Please change your mind; let her come down there with Charlie. Tell me in your next letter.

Our gallant district attorney takes over his "well-earned" gubernatorial reins next Monday. And we understand that not only will we have to contend with Hanley as governor, but also Grayce as chairman of the board of parole. Too bad, for Grayce fought you so hard during the trial while he was assistant prosecutor. But the paper will find a way. I know the time is getting pretty long and things must look dark to you, but everybody here is moving mountains to get you out.

Joe and Bill and Lew are still on the trail of Limpy and think they've picked up a lead which may turn into something. I don't want to say too much and raise your hopes too high, but really it does look as though something may possibly come of this.

Joe is also thinking of changing our editorial policy in favor of the new administration if it

will help get you out. He's already talked with
Mr. Carney [*the publisher*], and though it will
make the paper look bad, after the way we've
fought tooth and nail with the D.A., both Carney
and Joe are ready to make the switch. Of course
there's the chance, however, that the new administration won't want our support, now that the battle is over and the other three local papers are at
least outwardly supporting the D.A. now. I'll let
you know how things look.

I've been wondering if you couldn't get some
information from the inmates. It's just barely
possible that some of them may have underworld
connections which would help you in proving your
innocence. I know that it sounds pretty crazy to
think that possible, but there's always that one
chance, and we mustn't overlook anything. . . .

The letter slips into a more tender vein, filled with
reminiscences and dreams of the future. In the letter Joyce lays all her hopes and plans, despairs and
agonies, bare to the eyes of the censors who see the
mail before I do.

I reflect on the words she has written, going over
the letter again and again, wringing each possible
meaning, every last crumb of love and affection, from
the typed lines. . . . She can come to see me; in her
closing lines she has set the date as a week from Saturday—eleven more days. They seem like an unend-
ingly long time to wait. But I'm thankful that the old
administration, in its closing days of power, made this
one gesture which means so much to both Joyce and
me.

And my mother—perhaps it has been cruel to keep her from visiting me. But somehow, until I read this letter, I've wanted to spare her from seeing me in a prison uniform—viewing me in my misery. Now that is different. I'll write my mother and tell her to come down for a visit.

But I feel that with the new administration going into office my chances of freedom have been greatly lessened. Why should they release me—I, who fought them as only a person can who hates them intensely, and who might, once he is released, unearth evidence which may topple them from their lofty perches? And there'll be no change in the editorial policy of the *Record* for my benefit—not if I can help it. Things do look very black, as Joyce said, but I can stick it out until the boys get to the bottom of the case and expose the whole rotten mess. With Grayce, the ex-assistant prosecutor, heading the parole board, there isn't much hope for me even from that direction. I can only wait and hope, trusting in Joyce and the boys on the paper.

6

ANOTHER day served. . . .

You stand here at the bars of your cell, waiting for the screws to complete the night count. The wait is interminable; yet you must stand at your door, one hand on the bars, until the bell rings.

A screw dashes by, counting aloud each inmate he passes. In a moment another screw rushes past. He too counts aloud, and a harassed frown of great responsibility clouds his face.

The minutes drag on. You want a smoke. You'd like to brush your teeth, wash your hands and face, remove your shoes. Your feet burn, and your back is breaking from the heavy work in the shop. If you could only sit down. But it shouldn't take long; the bell should ring any moment.

And then—hell's fire! The first screw passes your cell again, puffing audibly and counting aloud. His running mate is close behind him, red of face and swollen fat with importance. . . . The first count was wrong. You curse all the dumb screws that can't count to one hundred without making a mistake. A mighty groan rises profanely from the length of the cell hall. Again the minutes drag past.

Someone rattles his cell door. Another inmate whistles a long sharp note. Much cursing and yawn-

61

ing, shuffling and sighing, muttering and growling—
any one of which means the hole if the offender is
caught. . . . Much comment on screws in general.

A voice, breaking fast and loud to get it over with
before the owner is identified, shouts, "Ring the bell!
I'm here, you son-of-a-bitch!"

Instant pandemonium. The cell hall rocks. Cat-
calls, howls, whistles, screams, rattles. Shoes stamp
the hard concrete floors.

At last the bell rings. Silence immediately reigns
again, and the inmates leave the doors of their cells.
The screws dash madly about, trying to locate a rat
that will snitch on the disturbers. The officers' faces
burn with indignation. They take any breaking of a
rule as a personal affront. "Who," they seem to demand, "dares violate the sanctity of the silent system?"
But you know they couldn't say it exactly like that.
The words are too big, the thought too profound.

Then the night screw comes around with a light for
your pipe. You'll get one every half hour till 8:30.

Pete Kassock has been a guard in this prison for
fourteen years. During this time he has amassed four
or five bright sayings. He uses them on little or no
provocation and makes them fit the occasion. Carlisle
and Ludke work in our shop, and are forever running
up to Pete's desk, snitching and catering to him. And
though they never hear a civil word from Pete, they
continue trying to ingratiate themselves into his favor.
This gives the other inmates additional reason to de-

spise the pair. And because Pete realizes this, he permits them to hover near by, tossing them an occasional barbed sentence and basking in the glow of their vacant, set smiles. Perhaps, also, the fat little guard's tremendous vanity is appeased to some extent by their never-failing response to his well-worn comments.

At 11:50 A.M. and at 4:20 P.M., Pete blows a tin whistle and we line up at the wash bowls. When he stamps the floor of his raised platform with his cane, we may start washing. Then we change our clothes, hang our overalls on the clothes rack, line up in double file and wait for the power-house whistle to hoot, summoning us to our meals. Until we step from the shop, we must remain uncovered; but during the process of buttoning up, we wear our caps, our hands being otherwise occupied. Occasionally an inmate forgets himself and steps into line wearing his cap. Pete immediately pounces upon him.

"Take off that cap. Your ears might catch cold when you go outside."

The handshakers laugh. The flustered inmate embarrassedly removes the cap. Pete sways far back, smiles self-satisfiedly, and rolls his eyeballs up until only the whites show.

The first time I heard him make the remark, I smiled. The second time, I grinned feebly. The third, I groaned. Now I merely grit my teeth. Surprisingly, it's the little inconsequential things like that which drive some of the prisoners into insanity. . . . I can understand why.

If one of us leans against a pillar—"You don't need to hold that post up. It'll stand without you."

If one of us is ill, and wishes to go to the hospital for medicine—"I'm the guy that oughta go to the hospital. You cry babies make me sick."

If one of us asks to go to the tailor shop for a clean uniform—"Y' sleep in the alleys an' eat garbage on the outside, and when y' git in jail you're hollerin' fer clean pants."

Thus it goes, invariably, day after day, until we feel we're going nuts. The little things. . . . There are no big things to bother us, save our own predicaments.

One noon just after I came to Stony Point, I stepped into line without buttoning the top button of my coat.

"Button up that coat. You might catch cold when y' git outside."

I groaned and buttoned the coat. The handshakers laughed. Back went Pete's eyeballs. Mueller, immediately behind me, growled quickly, "God, you're funny. Why don't you go on the stage?"

Pete's eyeballs snapped back to normal. He bounced up and down like a pulpy little jumping-jack.

"Who said that? By Christ, somebody's goin' t' the hole!"

As he stood trying to pin it on me, Red shouted, "I said it, you rooster-faced old bastard! Watcha gonna do about it?"

Everyone but the handshakers nearly split trying to keep from laughing. Pete waddled about like a lunatic, trying to identify this new voice among seventy men.

And then, "Mueller was the first guy that hollered, an' Fargo Red was the guy that just hollered now."— Ludke.

"That's right, Pete. I seen 'em both."—Carlisle.

Mueller and Red both went to the hole. And Pete hasn't forgotten that my unbuttoned coat led directly to the attacks which so injured his vanity.

When we are sick or need some medicine or salve and ask Pete to enter our names for sick call, he not only makes the most of his opportunity to inform us that we make him sick, but also usually fails to enter our names. As a rule, three or four days are frittered away before we can go to the hospital—which, in here, is the same as a drugstore on the outside. And by that time, we're probably recovered.

Though Stacey, Red and I have one of the hardest jobs in the shop, Pete always reserves any extra work for us. This we must do after we've been piling twine fiber into three-hundred-pound bales and are hot and tired.

If we need anything at all—toilet paper for our cells, shoe laces, a new library card, or any of the things that must be ordered through the deputy warden's of-fice—Pete flies into a rage. If the runner brings a pass for some inmate, Pete without fail points in my direction so that I'll think the pass is for me. Then when I get in front of his stand, he roars and curses me for leaving my machine. He has a cute trick of keeping me standing in front of his desk with my arm raised for permission to change my clothes and go where the pass directs. Then after five minutes or so of ignoring me, I get a tongue-lashing and am sent back to the machine. On one occasion, he even had me change clothes, then flew into a rage and threatened to throw me in the hole. When I started to explain that I had only obeyed his orders, he picked up his cane and would have split my head open if I hadn't retreated in a hurry. And of course he sends Red and Stacey and me to court so often that we lose our privileges at least once a month. We break the rules often enough by talking, but Pete doesn't catch us at it. He seems to realize, however, with the cunning of a madman, that we suffer much more intensely if our privileges are taken for something we haven't done.

But of the myriad methods he uses to produce insanity in us, his trait of keeping us standing for five or ten minutes when we want to visit the latrine is the most agonizing. We are not permitted to leave our positions without first obtaining Pete's consent. To do so, we must raise our hand and wait for Pete to nod his head. If we leave without permission, it may mean a trip to the hole. And it seems to please him to see Red, Stacey, Mueller, Lassiter or me dancing from one foot to the other, hand aloft like a school kid, as we await his grudging nod. He is a little czar, a petty Napoleon, who looks over us, under us and through us, but never at us. . . . I lie awake nights thinking of the stories I'll write about him, the tortures I'll inflict, when I'm free. I get a sort of lustful satisfaction out of the process. But deep in my heart, I know I'll never write anything or do anything.

Three months ago, we hoped that Mueller had cured Pete of his favorite pastime. It cost Mueller his second trip to the hole in less than a month and Pete's undying enmity. But it all went for nothing. Pete returned to his old ways before Mueller was out of third grade.

Mueller had been suffering from constipation and had taken guarded doses of laxative but without result. At last in desperation he appealed to Pete, who blandly administered a gigantic dose of Epsom salts. Combined with Mueller's former medicines, the salts had a powerful effect. But when Mueller raised his hand to visit the latrine, Pete affected not to see him. Mueller waved his hand violently for eight or nine minutes, and then, unable to stand it any longer, dashed to the scale, snatched a six-pound weight from the rack, and, running across the shop, hurled the heavy iron through the window at Pete's back.

"Now, you son-of-a-bitch," screamed Mueller, "do you see me?"

After that failed to change Pete, we figured we'd just have to go on as we were. But Stacey thought out a way to defeat Pete. The deputy warden or one of his assistants makes the rounds of the shops every half hour to see that all's well. During the minute or so that he's surveying the shop, Pete is very diligent. We choose this time to raise our hand. And now we never have to wait over a few seconds for Pete's nod.

His glare, however, when we pass the stand is murderous.

Lately he has been making life especially unbearable for Mueller—probably because of the weight-throwing incident and the day when Mueller hollered at him in line. Mose says that Carlisle and Ludke told Pete about Mueller's undying hatred. And that doesn't help Mueller any. Pete is continually sneaking up on Mueller's machine, in hope of catching Mueller or Lassiter, who works with him, in some infraction of the rules. . . . Both Lassiter and I fear that a showdown between Pete and Mueller is not far off.

Pete despises a convict, regardless of blood ties or good deeds performed in the past. His nephew served a term here, or so rumor has it, and when he was released, an orphan and nearly penniless, he went to Pete's home for help, but was turned away. . . . At another time, a little Jewish lawyer named Cohen was sent down here for five years on an extortion charge. A few years previously, Pete's brother had been jumped by a thug and would have been killed if Cohen hadn't happened to be passing and helped him beat off the thug. On the first day that Cohen was in the shop, Pete got down from his stand and talked with him. He told Cohen one of his pointless jokes, and Cohen, thinking that Pete was trying to make it easy for him because he'd saved Pete's brother, laughed. When Pete climbed back on the stand, Cohen smiled again, just to make Pete think he appreciated the joke. Pete promptly sent him to court for smiling, and Cohen lost his privileges for a week.

Life is never dull or prosaic when you work for Pete. But I don't think we'll have him with us long. A cloud is gathering on his horizon, and so swollen is he with his own importance that he fails to realize what may lie ahead. . . . If Mueller's application for pardon is denied, I'm afraid that Pete's suddenly going to learn that even a convict is more easily handled if a little kindness is used. But then it may be too late for Pete.

7

It is Sunday morning, and we stand at our cell doors, waiting for the gong to summon us to the motion picture show. We dare not leave the bars, for if we are late in stepping from our cells we lose our privileges.

Another week is gone. Time's battalions of seconds and minutes tick slowly away. The days and weeks tramp by without variation. The Sundays are twenty-four hours of misery, indistinguishable from the week days, save that we haven't even the solace of work to occupy our minds. For were we denied the privilege of working, we'd all soon be in the insane asylum.

Each weekday we rise at 6:40, clean our cells, eat breakfast in silence and march to the shops. At noon we return to the dining hall, talk between mouthfuls for twenty minutes, then file silently back to work. At 1:30 the passes are issued for all inmates who have been reported for infractions of the rules during the past twenty-four hours. They go to the deputy warden's office and are either given a demerit mark, excused on rare occasions, or put in the hole. At 4:30 the day ends. We eat our supper and are locked in our cells for the night—one man to a cell, which is a blessing. Some study, some read, but most merely sit and stare at the wall, growing daily more bitter and hateful. The night officer passes with a carbide lamp every half hour, for we are allowed no matches—possession of them means an immediate trip to the hole. If we want to smoke, we must roll up a piece of paper and set it on the cross-bars of the door. The officer touches his torch to it. The last light comes by at 8:30. At 9 o'clock the bell rings three long peals. Then we must undress promptly and be in bed in ten minutes, when the lights go out in the cells. Then we lie in the semi-darkness, staring out at the lighted corridor or up into the somber shadows of the ceiling, and think. Flights of fancy, hopes, memories carry us abroad for hours. Then at last we go to sleep, and once again we live and move in a free world—the fantastic world of dreams. . . . Sleep . . . There is nothing so good as sleep. . . .

Sunday morning, waiting for the bell. . . .

We contemplate the weeks and months that have slipped into the past, and our spirit faints. Here we accomplish nothing. And though we may be unjustly imprisoned or more than sufficiently punished, we know that there are many dreary months, perhaps years, ahead. Time drags slowly past, like camels plodding across a hot desert. There is nothing for us but hopes or plans or scenes from a past that is growing dim.

Sunday morning, and I hear Mueller on one side of me, Lassiter on the other, wearily shuffling their feet. . . . Then at last the bell rings, simultaneously informing the officers of all three cell halls that the motion picture is ready to be shown. The brass gong clangs four times; the cell doors on gallery four slide open. Silently we file down the railed cat-walk, descend the stairs and form two abreast on the tile flagging of the ground floor. The gong sounds three times, then twice, then once, as each gallery empties, and the line tramps from the north cell hall into the rotunda, where the inmates of the south cell hall merge with our file and march four abreast down the long arcade which leads to the auditorium, the inmates of the east cell hall, where the night crew sleeps, falling in at the rear of the line.

The inmate band is in the pit, blaring a familiar tune. I search my mind as my feet co-ordinate with the music. A marching piece—memories of tramping feet and cheering crowds and rifles and brave banners. *The Stars and Stripes Forever.* For no reason at all, I get a thrill. Wondering somewhat sheepishly if I am getting soft, I slide into a seat between Mueller and Lassiter.

Mueller, who is in the aisle seat, holds his nose at a passing inmate. Immediately a chorus of "phews." The passing inmate is Ludke, the rat. He takes an aisle seat a few rows down. The man beside him draws himself far away and holds his nose. Stacey slips into an aisle seat directly across from Ludke. The auditorium fills; the screws, who have been standing in the aisles, take their seats—one to about every fifteenth row.

The lights go out; a scratching sound, something like radio static, issues from the screen. The inmate orchestra lay aside their instruments. The title of the picture flashes on the screen. Symphonic music, played in accompaniment to the sub-titles, fades and is supplanted by ringing chimes. Big Ben . . . London . . . Midnight. . . . I fish a chocolate bar from my coat pocket and divide it with Mueller and Lassiter. They whisper thanks as their groping hands touch the candy. But there is no danger of our being seen. It is so dark that Mueller and Lassiter are like shadows against a black wall. A torrent of sound is issuing from the screen.

I settle back, chewing my chocolate, and prepare to get interested in the picture, but almost before it starts, a faint cough rises from the seats ahead. Unconsciously I tense. I cannot fathom the cause of my uneasiness until the thought suddenly smites me that Stacey and Ludke are seated ahead there in the darkness. . . . I try to peer into the gloom, but it is like trying to see through a blanket.

Two or three seconds drag by. My mind races. For I know. I know just as surely as I know that the sun will rise tomorrow. That sound was Ludke. . . . My nostrils catch a subtle odor of blood.

Then—a long, gurgling scream and someone crying, "Jesus Christ!" Something thumps against the floor, feet scrape, and a vague shadow rises black against the screen and stumbles into the aisle.

"Lights! For Christ's sake, turn on the lights!"

The lights flash on. Several guards rush to the inmate in the aisle.

"That guy!" he cries, pointing to the floor beneath Ludke's seat. "He chokes an' screams an' flops all over me! Lookit the blood on my clothes! My hands—— Oh, Jesus!"

All the inmates scramble to their feet. Ludke's seat is vacant. But I see a shoe sticking out into the aisle. The shoe twitches a little and then is still. A guard bends over and tugs at something beneath the seat. Then he straightens. He is very pale. He looks at his fingers. They are red. He stands to one side, staring frozenly at the floor and scrubbing at his hands with a handkerchief.

Deputy Armstrong charges down from the rear of the auditorium. He orders two inmates to drag Ludke from between the rows of seats. The men pick him up and heave him out into the aisle. He lands with a sickening smack. The deputy curses the inmates for roughness. They are a couple of lifers, solid parties that don't know what the word snitch means. The deputy kneels over Ludke and tugs at a knife which is buried deep in the right side of his neck. The deputy cannot release it. He listens for a heartbeat and examines Ludke's eyes. Then he rises.

"Take him to the hospital."

The two lifers grab Ludke's arms and legs. They do not hurry; there is no need. They mope up the aisle, very pleased and very slowly, giving everyone a chance to see their burden. Ludke's rump slaps against the floor at each step, leaving a smudge of blood that has seeped down from his neck. His eyes are open. His face is soft and harmless. As the lifers carry him past me, I tear my eyes from the handle of the knife . . . It looks familiar. I shudder. It's been a long time since I've seen a dead man.

Armstrong roars, "Everybody down in his own seat!"

Extra guards commence to pour down the aisles. They order, "Take the seat you had during the show." I notice that some of the night screws are on duty. They must have been called and got here in a hurry. Evidently they've been trained for just such an emergency as this.

I sink into my seat. Not until I am down do I realize my weakness. I seek out Stacey. He sits nonchalantly eying a pool of blood in the aisle.

Now Armstrong is questioning all the inmates that sat near Ludke. The men step into the aisle singly, where, after their hands have been examined for blood stains, they are searched. As soon as the deputy asks a round of questions, each man is led away by an officer. The inmate who sounded the cry is evidently absolved of complicity. The nature of the wound made it almost impossible for him to have inflicted it. He sat on Ludke's left. The knife entered from the right. . . . The deputy questions the fellow, and then he is led away by a guard.

When the deputy indicates Stacey, my heart pounds faster. But Stacey rises imperturbably and extends

his hands.   Only a handkerchief is found in his pockets.   He answers the deputy's questions and an officer
leads him away. . . . As he passes me, he smiles
tightly and winks.

The deputy's face is glistening with sweat.   He is
following a dangerous course.   The inmates are in
an uproar and the guards cannot quiet them.   Rules
against talking have ceased to exist.   Mueller and Lassiter excitedly hurl questions at me but answer themselves in high, hoarse shouts.

Armstrong grinds relentlessly on.

"Name and number."

"Carlisle, 100,888."

"What do you know about this?"

"Nothing."

"Mean to say you were sitting right there near him
and didn't see a thing?"

"It was too dark; I was watchin' the pitcher."

"We'll find ways to make you smart guys talk. . . .
Take him away."

There is fear in Carlisle's eyes when he marches past
our seats.

But the deputy is getting no place.   The knifing of
Ludke has at least temporarily put the fear of God into
Carlisle and the rest of his kind.   Nobody heard a
thing; nobody saw anything; nobody knows anything.

Someone in the rear of the auditorium yells, "For
Christ's sake, shut off that God-damn pitcher!"

All of the inmates take up the cry.   Someone howls,
"Yeow!   They bumped one o' the rats!" . . . An-

other shouts, "Bump 'em all, the dirty——" One man
starts to stamp his feet. In a moment, the auditorium
reverberates, as though from thunder. As a precaution against open rioting, we are herded to our cells.

I sit on my cot and think: "Well, it's really your
fault. You knew all along they were going to bump
him. And if you'd tipped the deputy, Ludke'd be alive
right now. And maybe you'd be going home to Joyce
and your mother on a pardon. Maybe it's not too late.
Joyce and Bill and Lew'll never find Limpy now or
unearth any new evidence. Too long ago. Everybody's forgotten about it. You'll have to do your
time. Unless you snitch. Then maybe you'll get a
pardon. . . . If you were on the outside, you'd never
cover up a murder. You'd run the whole story down
and slap it all over the front page."

Then I realize for the first time that I've acquired
the mind of a convict. "But you aren't on the outside.
You're in the stir now, and they think you're just as
guilty and just as rotten as anybody else in here. And
you're no rat. No, by God. These cons are your
friends. They trust you. . . . Besides, the world is
better off without people like Ludke.

"But——

"Oh, the hell with it."

Four days have passed, and the mystery of Ludke's
death is unsolved. The prison and county authorities have run into a wall of silence. The finks are

afraid to talk, and the rest of the inmates will not break their one inflexible rule: "Don't rat."

Stacey seems happier than I've ever seen him before. An amused little smile crinkles the corners of his eyes, and he hums softly as he goes about his work.

8

I GLANCE toward the shop guard's platform and see the inmate runner from the visiting room hand a pass to Pete. He motions to me, but I figure it's another one of his tricks to get me in front of the stand so he can humiliate me, and I pretend not to see him. He waves his arms violently in my direction and starts pounding the platform with his cane—not that the noise can be heard in the din of the roaring machines. Fargo Red taps my shoulder and points to Pete. I simulate surprise and step from the box as Red takes my place. Pete's face is purple with anger, and he is yelling and rolling his eyes. I wipe the sweat from my face and shoulders, take off my overalls and don my shirt and uniform. Pete flings the pass at me.

"Visit!" he howls above the clash of the machinery. "An' you try that smart business o' makin' off yuh don't see me agin, an' I'll park your lazy fanny in that hole!"

I finger the pass in dismay. My mother and my brother are here to see me. It is their first visit. My hands start to tremble; my throat is dry. They are here. All their lives they'll remember me as they see me today in my ill-fitting prison uniform, my clod-hopper shoes, my misery. But I am thankful for one thing. This morning we were given our weekly shave. At least my face is smooth and clean.

"Well," bellows Pete, "what the hell yuh waitin' fer?"

I leave the shop, march across the prison yard and ascend the steps of the long arcade which joins the dining hall and the auditorium at one end with the three cell halls and the offices. I pass the night crew's cell hall, where five hundred men are now asleep. And there is the bathroom, where we bathe, fifty at a time, each week. There is the deputy warden's office, with its solid steel door in the farther wall which opens into the solitary and the detention ward. The deputy and the captain of the solitary are leading an inmate through the door that opens into the hole as I pass. . . . I continue down the hall. There is the tailor shop, where, endless ages ago, I was led naked from the deputy warden's office. The heavy odors of steam and strong yellow soap penetrate the hall from the laundry at the rear of the tailor shop. And then I am passing the print shop, to which, each week, I send copy for the little prison paper. There is the library, with its thousands of volumes. And then I am passing into the great rotunda, with the north cell hall and the south cell hall, housing over fifteen hundred inmates each, opening on either side. I cross the rotunda and halt in front of the gates.

The first of the four gates stands open. The turnkey motions me through it and directs me to face the wall and wait. I obey, folding my arms and resting my forehead against the dark yellow bricks. Such is the procedure. I must not turn around until my name

is called, which may be in a minute or an hour, depending upon the number of visitors ahead of my
mother and my brother.   For only ten visitors are
allowed in the visiting room at a time, and each visit
is under the supervision of a guard who sits with the
visitors. . . . At my back is the officers' barber shop,
which serves during the day as the visiting room.

Hoping the turnkey won't see me and send me to
court, I take a chance and glance around quickly.   The
gate of the visiting room is open, and the three barber
chairs are shrouded in sheets and drawn back against
the far wall.   One officer is seated in the room.   He
sits perfectly still, his head hanging and his hands
clasped, and stares sleepily at his shoes.   There are
no other guards or visitors in the room.   I shan't have
long to wait. . . . And my mother and brother and I
shall at least be alone with the guard.

The turnkey, whose desk stands between the second
and the third gates, calls me.

"Ross!   You wanna take a trip to court?"

I swing around.   "No."

"Then cut out that staring at the visitors' room. . . .
Face that wall. . . . And say 'sir' when you address
an officer."

I blink, say "yessir," and am properly grateful. The
turnkey's bite isn't as bad as his bark.   He could have
reported me and cost me my privileges.

I stand close to the wall, shifting from one foot to
the other.   One leg goes to sleep.   I start counting the
bricks in front of me.   There is sand sprinkled on the

floor underfoot—white sand, which keeps the inmates from scratching and dirtying the tile floor. Every place an inmate must stand and wait in Stony Point, there's the inevitable sprinkling of white sand. . . . I try to form a pile with the point of my shoe. . . . And I wonder if any word is being brought by my mother from Joyce or the boys at the office.

And then—"All right, Ross. In the visiting room."

I about-face and enter the visiting room. The officer snaps out of his lethargy and asks how many visitors I have, then arranges straight-back chairs—three against the wall and one facing the three. The latter he indicates is mine.

I sit down. He examines my pass, mutters, "Mother and brother, hey?" scrawls his initials upon the back and warns me to return it to Pete. Then he hauls a big gold watch from his pocket and records the time. . . . He will see that my visit doesn't go beyond the half hour limit. Neither of us speaks further.

A lock rattles; a gate opens and clangs shut. A second rattle, a second clang. A third—I peer through the bars of the visiting room. A young boy stands just inside the open gate. That will be Charles, my little brother. He is frightened. His eyes are large. His face is white. . . . My cheeks burn, and I lower my head. Then I glance up again. Yes, it is my little brother.

He sees me. "Frank!"

Numbly I nod and try to get to my feet, but my legs are putty, my arms leaden weights.

Charles edges toward me, then stumbles back to the open gate.

"Mother, here is Frank."

I fix my gaze on the tips of my shoes. I grit my teeth, clench my fists, but the floor, the shoes, the legs of the chairs—all swim in a pool of mist. I blink my eyes—Mother, here is Frank.

My mother's slow steps pass through the gate and enter the visiting room. Slowly I glance up. She moves with difficulty, as though she is fighting against faintness. Charles guides her to a chair. She seats herself at the guard's right; Charles sits at his left.

My mother's face is set and white. She is like a person who has been dazed by some horrible accident. In her hands is an aluminum tray, furnished by the prison, and on the tray is a cardboard box, like the kind that comes from bakeries. I hitch my chair a little nearer to her. She offers me the tray. My lips commence to tremble. . . .

I try to accept the tray, but my hands refuse to obey me. I can only drop my glance and stare miserably at the floor. Fiercely I grind my teeth. Words swell within me, but I can utter only hoarse, croaking sounds. My sight dims.

Charles whispers, "Mother, Frank is crying."

Somehow one of my hands reaches his knee and fumblingly pats him. He is so young. Once I was young and wore knee pants. . . . Mother, Frank is crying. . . . That is my little brother.

But my movement breaks the spell. I get out my big red bandana handkerchief and scrub savagely at my eyes. My sight clears. I see my mother plainly. She is old—old. Her hands tremble as she extends the tray. I set it upon my knees, and kiss her hand.

"It's good of you to come. But you shouldn't—the one-hundred-mile bus ride over the mountains, the strain on your heart, the expense——"

Her eyes are searching me, as if they can probe out any hurts or ailments that are hidden. "You are well?" Her voice is a strained whisper.

"Yes, I'm all right."

She is very pale, very slight. She has lost much weight, and seems like a wisp of fragile gentleness, her little black hat and her dark coat intensifying the whiteness of her face. So great is her suffering, she is beyond tears.

"Your face is so thin and pale," she says. "You're sure you're all right?"

"Yes, Mother. I feel fine."

"Are they good to you here? You aren't suffering?"

"No, Mother. I'm not suffering."

"Do you get plenty of good food?"

"Yes."

My imprisonment causes my mother much more suffering than it does me. A nerve constantly twitches in her throat.

"You've never mentioned your work in your letters," she says. "Is it terribly hard?"

Here I have learned to lie convincingly if nothing else.

"No, the work is easy. I've got a swell job. The easiest in the place. All I have to do is keep track of the twine stock and write little articles and stories for the prison paper."

The officer smiles benignly and nods.

"Yes," my mother says, "I'm so glad to get the paper. It's just like having an extra letter from you each week." She is thoughtful for a moment. Then, "But being locked up, in a cell each night—my heart bleeds for you, my child."

"You mustn't worry. Everything's all right."

"I'm glad. I've been so worried."

"I've got to get out of here," I cry. "They've got to let me come home! Every day I see men go—criminals with plenty of money and the right kind of outside influence. I haven't done anything. Can't they see this was a frame?"

"If your father were only alive——"

"But you're not well. They're punishing both of us for something I didn't do."

"My poor boy. There never was a better boy."

"Can't anything be done? Didn't you bring any word from Joyce or Bill or Lew?"

"Joyce is coming to see you tomorrow. We thought you'd rather see her alone. But she said that they were on the trail of this crippled man in California. A boy who used to work with you on the Associated Press is out there, and he's making an investigation. They think that if they can find this crippled man, they'll have the case settled."

"No. I only had a hunch that Limpy was there that night. . . . And maybe, even if he really was there," I add, hating the thought, "Limpy didn't see what happened. And if the boys do find him, maybe he won't be able to help. . . . But if he did see it, chances are he didn't even know the men. They're probably from out of town."

"But I'm sure you'll go free," says my mother. "If the paper can't do anything, the pardon board will when you apply to them."

"I can't apply again till next year, and I'm afraid there's so much time passed now that the boys won't be able to find out anything anyway. . . . And it's a cinch if the paper's unable to do anything for me, I'll just be wasting a lot of effort by going before that pardon board again. . . . You know that the Governor's the chairman, and he was the prosecutor in my case. . . . A dirty thief if there ever was one."

"You shouldn't say that. You don't know."—My mother.

"Is there any hope at all?"

"We stopped at the capitol when we changed buses. The Governor couldn't see me, but his secretary sent us to the parole board. I talked with the chairman. He said he couldn't promise anything—that it's up to the other members of the board as much as it is to him."

"Where does he get that stuff?" I cry. "I've seen what goes on around here."

The guard eyes me, starts as if to say something, then sits back.

"You must be patient. Mr. Campbell says we're bucking the worst case he's ever seen. He says that it's going to be a long, hard row to hoe before we break the forces that put you here. . . . If it takes a lot longer, I'm sure the parole board will be just and fair with you when you're eligible."

Six months before I'm eligible—six months more. And then?

"Do you think I'll get a parole first time up?"

"You will if God hears my prayers."

My mother still believes that an almighty God watches over His flock and corrects the errors of its leaders.

"And mine," whispers Charles. "I pray for you too."

He lowers his head and a big tear splashes against his coat sleeve. Last year I took him to the circus. We watched the animals and the clowns and the acrobats. Charles drank five glasses of lemonade and was sick. And now—I pray for you too. . . . My little brother.

My mother plucks at the strings around the pastry box.

"You must eat your lunch. I brought everything you like: strawberry shortcake, chicken, nut bread, oatmeal cookies, ice cream. I got the ice cream at a little store across the road from the prison. Did you know there's a store there?"

"I guess I didn't pay much attention to things when I was brought down here."

"An old, old man runs it.   He said that most of the visitors buy their ice cream from him.   I was going to get you a bottle of milk, but he said the warden won't allow liquids to be brought in."

I open the box.   For months I have dreamed of such food as this.   But now I am without appetite. My stomach is a leather sack, my palate incapable of tasting.   But I must make some pretext of eating.

"You shouldn't have brought so much."   If I could only take the food to my cell——   But no.   The prison rules again.   "It's too good for me," I add.   "I'm used to plain food now.   A sandwich would have been plenty."

But she is pleased, so I nibble at the chicken and swallow some of the ice cream.   A hole has been scooped in the top and chocolate syrup poured in. . . . The old, old man across the road——   I prevail upon Charles to help me eat the lunch.

Over and over I tell myself, "This is your mother; this is your brother."   Yet I cannot believe it.   I seem to be someone who is sitting in the background watching the scene being enacted.   I cannot be a part of it. A veil hangs between us.   I am no longer the same Frank Ross who was a son and a brother.   I have lost all track of everything that is good and fine.   Imprisonment has atrophied me.   I sneer at God and church, and despise all weaklings who seek divine guidance.   The Bible is a collection of inane tales, told by a cracked, unknown, fanatical mind which was steeped in the ignorance and superstitions of the Dark

Ages. . . . Prison has done that for me. . . . I feel
like an old, worn boiler, whose plating is cracked and
whose warmth has long ago seeped away. Nothing
holds my interest for more than a moment. . . . At
times I fear that I am lost.

I can pretend with the food no longer. I set the
tray on the floor. My mother catches my hand.

"Frank, you must tell me. You must." Her fears
deepen the lines in her face. "Something is wrong.
You can't even eat the things you like best. And I
imagine so many terrible things, knowing nothing.
Tell me; it will be easier for me if I only know—is it
so awfully bad here?"

"Please don't worry, Mother. There are lots worse
places than this."

"But Charles got a book from the library that was
all about prison. It was terrible—terrible. They tied
the prisoners to the bars and beat them with straps."

Ah, Mother, Mother—they tied the prisoners to the
bars and beat them with straps. Shall I tell you about
Stony Point, where they chain the prisoners to the bars
of the solitary and beat them not with straps but with
canes or blackjacks? Shall I tell you about Cava-
naugh, whom I saw knocked down and kicked all the
length of the long arcade? About little Mantecas, a
Mexican who couldn't even understand English, and
who was caned to death by a guard because he
misunderstood the guard's instructions? Shall I tell
you that the killing was covered—that the guard still
works here? Shall I tell you about Reed, who was

chained to the bars and beaten until his skull was fractured in three places, and who died in solitary confinement, his death reported to the board of control as accidental? About Pete Kassock? About Ludke? About Carlisle? About the hospital treatment? About the days and weeks and months of maddening silence? About the screams and moans and cries of sleeping prisoners at night? Shall I tell you about the men who hang themselves in their cells, the men who eat ground glass, the men who drink nicotine-poisoned water, the men who fling their bodies from the third and fourth galleries when the cells are unlocked in the mornings, gladly accepting a horrible and violent death rather than trying to rehabilitate themselves? . . . No, no, Mother. You must never know. I cannot tell you.

"That was only a book," I say. "Authors always exaggerate."

I had imagined that a visit would be different from this—that it would be a few minutes of joy. Yet we, the Rosses, lapse into silence and experience only sorrow, unable to summon even an empty smile, unwilling to reminisce over happier days, lest we break utterly. But perhaps there can be little joy in this room. Its walls have witnessed too much sorrow.

And the minutes are fleeting; the visit is nearing its end. Already the guard has glanced at his watch. The minute hand is close to the half-hour mark.

But what is there that we can say? Banalities are beyond us. The thoughts closest to our minds must be crowded down lest they overwhelm us. We can merely slump lower in our seats and blink back the mists.

The officer touches my knee and snaps shut his watch. A half hour has passed; the visit has ended.

"I must go now, Mother."

The officer says, "You can't get up yet, lady. He's got to leave the room first." Rules, rules——

My mother catches my hand.

"Write as often as you can. I feel that I'd die if I didn't know how you were."

"I'll write every time I can—either to you or Joyce."

"Yes, Joyce is such a comfort to me."

"Good-by, Mother."

"Be brave, my son. Remember, God is watching over you."

"I will, Mother. Good-by."

"And go to church every Sunday."

"I will, Mother. Good-by."

"And obey the rules. Keep your record clean."

That is my mother speaking—obey the rules; keep your record clean. I am not a man. I am just her little boy, who yesterday learned to walk, and strayed too far, and crawled back to her to nurse his hurts.

"I will, Mother. Good-by."

"I shall pray for you every night, my son."

Now the tension and fear have passed somewhat and she is sobbing softly. She seems desperately frail.

"Take good care of Mother, Charles. And be a good boy."

I hold my little brother's hand for a moment, then kiss my mother's cheek. It is cold and wet; her eyes are clouded with unhappy mists, and her body trembles. There is so much left unsaid; yet, even if we were granted additional time, we should be unable to say it.

"Good-by, Mother . . . Charles . . ."

"Good-by . . . Good-by. . . ."

I rise and pass through the rotunda. Gates rattle and slam. I glance around. My mother and my brother, two silhouettes against the outside door, are moving through the last gate. Then the front door opens and they leave the prison.

I stumble past the deputy's office, down the steps of the arcade and start across the prison yard. I blink my eyes and scuff at a leaf on the concrete walk. . . .

9

STACEY saunters to the rear end of the breaker and, ducking from sight, motions to me. I take a look toward Pete's stand. He is busy bawling out Lassiter and doesn't see me, so I drop down behind the breaker and crawl over to Stacey. Red stands guard so Pete can't sneak up on us.

"You got people on the outside, ain't you?" asks Stacey. "A mother or something?"

I nod. "Mother and brother. They were just here on a visit."

"Old man's dead?"

"Yes."

"Any dough?"

I shake my head.

"That paper you worked for doing you any good?"

"No. They're against the administration. The paper can't help me."

"Tough. . . . A bum rap, wasn't it?"

I nod, then ask, "What's all this for?"

"You could get out easy enough if you wanted to. I suppose you've thought of that plenty—thought of how you'd be able to track down the guys that framed you then."

I say cautiously, "What makes you think that?"

"Listen, Frank, you've got me where the hair's short.

93

You know it, and I know it. You saw that shiv, you
saw where I was sitting, and you know damn well who
bumped Ludke. You've known all along. A word
from you and I'd be doing the book in the hole and
you'd probably be pardoned."

I wet my lips. The same thought has passed through
my mind many times. So far I've managed to stifle it.

"Forget it," I gulp. "I don't know anything. . . .
Besides I'm no rat."

"No, I'm not forgetting it. You had a chance to
put me on the spot and get yourself out of a jam all at
the same time, but you kept your mouth shut. You're
solid. I owe you plenty for that."

"You don't owe me anything."

"I owe you, and now I'm gonna pay. . . . Kid, did
you ever think that if I was outta here I could find out
damn quick who framed you and get you sprung?"

"How?"

"With the connections I've got outside, I can find
out anything that's happened in the underworld. I can
put dough in the right places and get anything done.
I can even have the guys brought in that framed you.
But I've got to get out to do it. Yours is a tough rap,
and I couldn't handle outside parties from in here."

I smile. "Then all we've got to do is get you out
of here."

"That's right where you come in. If you'll help me
now, I'll get out, and you can rest damn sure that you'll
be out too—just as quick as I can work it."

It all sounds a little bewildering—and, too, I'm afraid Stacey is having one of the pipe dreams that sometimes set the inmates to scheming impossible things. I decide to humor him along.

"Where do I fit in?" I ask. But something in my voice must tell him that I haven't any confidence in whatever scheme he has spun.

"Listen, kid." He grabs my arm. "This is no screwy idea I'm telling you. This is the goods—your one chance to get out of this joint on a clean pardon with the whole damn frame-up uncovered. . . . You helped me once when you surprised me with that knife and kept your mouth shut. Now you help me again and I'll help you."

The lights flashing in his eyes show me that he's really in earnest—that he really has something.

"Okay, Stacey. Shoot."

"Well, in the first place, I didn't bump that rat punk, Ludke, just because I wanted to get rid of him for ratting on me. I'm not so nuts I'd risk the book in the hole just to get rid of a rat. I had a damn good reason for killing that fink, and it's because I killed him that I'm going to be able to beat this joint."

I am in more of a muddle than ever. "You'd better begin at the start, Stacey," I say helplessly.

"All right. If you kill somebody in here, they take you down to the county seat and put you on trial. I'm doing life, so my only chance to get out of here is to go to the county seat and try it from there. A guy couldn't get over these walls in a million years. . . .

Remember Garsky who went out a while back? He and I figured this out: I kill Ludke. Then to avoid suspicion, it rides along for a while. Then I let somebody find out about it and he snitches to the deputy. By that time, Garsky's time's up and he's on the outside. He follows the case through the papers or through a mouthpiece. He knows what day I'm to be brought to court. He knows what courtroom I'll be in. So he arranges everything for the getaway. . . . It's so simple I'm surprised nobody thought of it before."

"But," I object, "it'd take an army to get you out of that courthouse. A lot of guys have tried it, but everyone's been killed or captured."

"They tried it alone, after they'd killed some guy when they were crazy mad. They didn't plan it before the killing. . . . I'm not gonna tell you just how we're gonna work this, but it's so simple it can't miss. And then I'll get right to work on this case of yours. . . . Those newspaper guys and that girl okay? All right, then, I'll get in touch with them as soon as I have something for them to work on."

· "What'll I do?"

"Tell the deputy just what you know—about the shiv; identify it; about seeing me practicing with it; about Ludke ratting. Put the finger right smack on me. Make him think you're trying to help yourself."

"No," I decide. "There'll be some shooting down at the courthouse probably if Garsky's going to take you out of there, and I don't want any more blood on

my hands. . . . I could have stopped you from killing
Ludke if I'd used my head.   It's been on my mind a
lot."

"Listen.   I'll give you my word, and you know I
don't lie.   There won't be any gunplay in this.   It
won't be needed.   You've got to take my word for it."

"But," I object, "I'll have to come back here after
you're gone, and all the guys'll think I'm a rat."

"The hell with that noise.   I'll square you with
every right guy in the joint, and what do you care
what those finks and farmers think of you?   It'll only
be for a little while anyway.   Then you'll be out and
the guys that put you here'll be in."

The offer is tempting—if I were only sure no one
would be killed.

"You'll give me your word nobody's going to get
hurt?"   I ask.

"My word of honor as a con."

He is solemn.   There is no gag meant.   I can't
doubt him.

"Okay, Stacey.   I'll sail with you. . . . After all,
I want out just as bad as you."

"Don't go in this with your eyes closed, Ross.   You
may have to take a hell of a lot of misery, after I'm
gone and you're back here.   The warden may figure
you had a hand in my lamming and beat hell out of you
and throw you in the hole.   But I'll get you out, kid,
and a lot quicker than you'll ever get out if you wait on
the parole or pardon board, standing the way you do
with the administration."

"I won't mind the abuse, as long as I get out."

Stacey is thoughtful for a moment. He peers over the top of the machine. Fargo Red shuts it off as the last three-hundred-pound-bale is finished, walks back to the tank and shuts off the oil, at the same time signaling us that all is clear. He grins and lines his jaws with snuff.

Stacey says, "But don't break down and confess, Ross. They can hang another seven years on you for helping me. So once it's done, keep your mouth shut. Don't admit helping me. Swear to Christ and back again you didn't know anything about it. . . . That's the tough part of this. I was going to let Carlisle overhear me talking about the killing or something like that so he'd snitch to the deputy and then get in bad when I'd got away. But you deserve a break for keeping still, and if you can take it for a while, I'll get you out. Remember that. No matter how black things look or if you have to wait a long time for me to get things done, I won't fail you. I'll get you out—legally. . . . I'd take you with me, from the courtroom, but, in the first place, it'll only work for one man, and in the second, you probably wouldn't go that way anyway."

I nod.

"After you've spilled to the deputy, he'll call me in there. If you're there, too, I'd better start a fight with you. It'll look better, because he's suspicious of everything and may think it's funny you started snitching all of a sudden."

"Okay. What'll I tell him?"

"Just tell him the truth—everything you know except that I admitted it to you, and of course don't mention this talk just now. As long as you stick to the truth, there's no chance of your getting jammed up when he starts pouring the heat on you."

"Shall I go right now?"

"Sure. Get a pass. Tell Pete it's about the Ludke killing, and he'll break his neck to get you over to Armstrong's office."

"All right, Stacey. Good luck."

"So long, kid." We shake hands. "Thanks for everything, and just sit tight till it's over. Stacey'll get you out."

I rise to get the pass, but then for the first time see the pasty face and beady eyes of Carlisle behind the manila and sisal piles in the rear of the shop. But he's too far back—couldn't possibly have heard us. Yet, he saw us shaking hands. . . . Stacey balls his fist, and the rat ducks to safety. Stacey shakes his head at me. "Okay. Don't worry about him. He didn't hear a word, and what he saw won't mean anything."

Now I am in Deputy Warden Armstrong's office. He is busy at his roll-top desk, writing. I stand just within the door, waiting for him to look up. Then he glances at me—a large, heavily-framed man with a red face and shaggy eyebrows. "What's on your mind?"

"It's something I know about the Ludke case."

He snaps erect in his chair. "Here. **Sit down.** . . . What do you know about Ludke?"

I tell him the entire tale, beginning with Stacey's knowing about Ludke having ratted on him for having a can of soda, about Stacey's knife-throwing ability, and about the knife I saw Stacey practicing with.

"Can you identify the knife?"

"Yes, sir."

"Did anybody else see it?"

"Not that I know of."

"Anybody hear Stacey make any **threats?**"

"I don't know."

"Why didn't you tell me this before?"

"I was afraid maybe I'd get killed too. But **my** conscience bothered me a lot, and I figured too that maybe I'd get a better break from the board."

Though the deputy tries to conceal it, I can see that he doesn't like rats and squealers. A few minutes ago, he eyed me impersonally but in a half-friendly fashion. Now he's all business, but acts as though he's closing a deal with someone he's suddenly taken a dislike to. . . . But I have to go through with it now.

"Well," he says, "it's only your word against his. But his record may convict him. Now that we have something to work on, the county attorney's office may be able to hang it on him."

He rises and steps to the door. "Send for Stacey," he orders. "Get him over here right away."

Stacey arrives in five minutes.

The deputy scowls at him and growls, "So you're the smart guy that didn't know anything about that Ludke killing!"

Stacey says nothing.

"You might as well come clean for once and make it easy for yourself," says the deputy. "We've got it on you, dead to rights."

Stacey merely shrugs. I feel a chill of apprehension. Little questions start to tick in the back of my mind. I tell myself that I should have thought this over before acting. Another day or two wouldn't make any difference, if Garsky is watching the papers and the calendar. . . . But there's nothing to be afraid of. Naturally Stacey isn't going to stand there and admit it. He's got to leave himself some out in case the escape plans fall through. And, besides, the deputy'd smell a rat if Stacey admitted the killing.

"Open that mouth," snarls the deputy, "before I knock you clear across the room."

Stacey's eyes are cold and lifeless. They rove from me to the deputy. "There ain't much to say."

"In other words, you admit it?"

Stacey doesn't reply.

"You might as well make a statement," insists the deputy. "You haven't got a chance."

Stacey's silence is maddening. And then at last he speaks, not to the deputy, but to me.

"You dirty scissor-bill! You lying rat! I'll get you for this if it's the last thing I ever do!"

His sudden lunge catches me unprepared. His fingers clutch at my throat, his legs trip me, and we roll into the corner. His lips are close to my ear.

"Nice work, kid."

We thrash about, putting on quite a battle. Then the deputy and some officers from the outer office charge at us, tear Stacey from me, and fling him into the opposite corner.

"I wouldn't have wanted a nicer confession," says the deputy. "Throw him in the hole."

The guards lead Stacey away. The deputy turns to me.

"Just keep quiet till we can get an indictment and drag that guy down to court for another trial. Don't talk around the yard too much, and watch out for yourself. . . . Some of these birds in here might not like the fact that we got our information from you."

"I know," I mutter unhappily. "You think I'm a rat. Well, I wouldn't cover up a murder on the outside, so I don't see why I should in here."

The deputy laughs and shakes his head. But I can read his eyes. He thinks that I've just brought misery to a man who is already even more miserable than I. Let him think. I've got plenty at stake, and no chance at freedom is too big to risk. But I don't need a fortune-teller to forecast the kind of jam I'm going to be in after Stacey escapes—if he makes it. . . .

"How long will it be before he goes to trial?" I ask.

"Maybe a month—maybe a week. Depends on his preliminary plea."

"Will I have to be in court?"

"Yes. The county attorney'll probably be down here soon to see you before the trial."

Someway, somehow, I've got to get word out to the paper concerning what is to happen. Not only must they know that Stacey is working with us, but also I can't let a beat like his escape go by without the *Record's* having a cameraman and reporter on hand to cover it. . . . And then I recall the old secret writing trick Joyce and I used at school.

"Deputy," I say, "I'm doing this thing for the prison and for the state. How about the state doing something for me?"

"What's that?"

"I want to send a special letter to my girl tonight."

He laughs. "I thought you were going to ask for a pardon. . . . Well, I don't know what the pardon board'll do for you when they hear of this, but I do know you'll find the paper and an envelope for a special letter on your cot tonight."

Back in the shop, Red motions me down behind the breaker and growls, "Where the hell you been?"

"I saw the deputy about sending a special letter tonight, and while I was there, they tossed Stacey in the hole."

"The hell! What for?"

"Can't say right now, but I'll try to find out something for you later. . . . Here's what I want now.

How can I get another letter—a secret one—out of this joint without the censors seeing it?"

"There's a screw that'll take them out for twenty-five bucks, but you got to have the cash."

"Will he collect from the other end?"

"He might.   I'll see and let you know in a couple of days."

"No, I've got to know right now and write the letter tonight."

"You're s. o. l. then."

"How about the old invisible ink gag, Red?   Do you think they ever heard of it here?"

"Invisible ink?   Where the hell you gonna get anything like that in this joint?"

"Lemon juice.   It doesn't show at all and works like a charm.   But what I want to know is, are they hep to it here?"

"Not that I heard of in the last seven years.   I never knew you could use that stuff.   And nobody in here ever used it as far as I know."

"Okay," I decide, "I'll take a chance on it then. First I'll write a regular letter; then I'll write between the lines. . . . What bothers me, though, is where I'm going to get the juice.   Can you score for some?"

"Sure, that's a cinch.   I'll send word over by Mose to Dale in the tailor shop.   Then he'll pass the word along to Pat O'Brien.   He works in the tailor shop too, but waits on table in the kitchen and eats early. He'll get the lemon juice and slip it to Billie, the run-

ner in the deputy's office, and Billie'll have the stuff
under your pillow tonight."

"My God," I gasp. "Does it have to go through
all those hands?"

"That's the only way we can get it unless you want
to wait till a week from Saturday."

"Okay, Red. You're a lifesaver."

The hairy man dips heavily into his can of snuff,
then drags out the inevitable plug.

"How about Stacey going to the hole, though?
Gimme the dope on that."

"I can't just yet, Red. When he wants you to know,
he'll send word out through Billie. But if you hear
anything about me in the meantime, don't pay any
attention to it."

Red regards me queerly, then rises and starts toward
Mose.

10

THE SPECIAL letter is on my cot when I reach my cell after supper. I stand at the cell door, waiting for the screws to make the night count, and wondering if the lemon juice is under my pillow as Red promised. . . . The wait is everlastingly long—the first count, as usual, is wrong, and must be made over again. . . . If I am caught trying to get the letter out, it will mean solitary confinement. True, the boys involved in obtaining the lemon juice would be given the same punishment if they were caught. But too much is at stake—my freedom, as well as a front page beat for the *Record*. I must take the chance. And if I'm caught, I'll take the rap alone; certainly I won't even think of implicating the others with me.

At last the bell rings, and I may leave my cell door. I fish under the pillow and heave a sigh of relief. The lemon juice is there—a small phial of it—enough for many a letter.

First I write conventionally to Joyce, then clean the pen point out well and start writing between the lines with lemon juice.

This is dangerous; never attempt it unless you've something terribly important to tell me.

You remember Stacey, the man who ran the underworld before he was arrested a couple of

106

years ago? He's going to escape within the next
month. He's up for murder at the county seat
of this county pretty soon and he's going to escape
from the courtroom. Have a cameraman and two
reporters there at the time. Stay away yourself. He's promised that there'll be no gunplay
or bloodshed, but I'm afraid to have you there
nevertheless. I'll be in the courtroom at the time.
Tell Bill and Lew or whoever else may cover the
story to talk the deputy into allowing them to
speak to me for a minute. I may be able to sneak
them a little more information. Watch the wire
reports for the date of Stacey's arraignment or
hearing.

After Stacey escapes, you'll hear from him.
He's going to trace down the people who framed
me and force a confession from them. He's one
of the really big shots in crime in this part of the
country. He can learn very easily who framed
me, if he can just get an inkling of who the person
was that actually made contact with the pair who
worked the frame. He'll work on Limpy for this
I hope. And, perhaps, the aldermen or the car
dealer. But he'll find out. Trust him to do that.
All he'll have to do is ask, and it will be like John
Dillinger asking who killed a deadly enemy of his.

When he gets in touch with you, do as he says.
Pass the word along to Bill and Lew and Joe.

Tomorrow, I'll see you. By the time this letter
reaches you, I'll already have held you in my arms
again. . . . Maybe after these months of separa-
tion and misery and trouble, it's all about to end.

I shan't risk writing like this any more unless
something of great importance arises.

I wait for the lemon juice to dry, then inspect the letter by the light in the ceiling of my cell. No trace of the invisible writing remains. I fold the letter, address the envelope in real ink, and give it to Mac when he passes my cell with the first light of the evening.

The cell is small—I can touch each side when I spread my arms. Lengthwise, it is only large enough for me to take three steps. And now I am pacing up and down, scheming for tomorrow when Joyce visits me and I must somehow inform her of the invisible writing; planning for the future, once Stacey escapes and helps me; fearing what may lie ahead for me here in prison, after Stacey is gone and if I am implicated. But there will be nothing definite which can tie me in with his escape. They may try to beat something out of me, once it is over, as Stacey said, but I'll just sit tight and keep my mouth shut.

I take three steps, pause, turn, then retrace my movements. On the wall is a steel locker for keeping my soap and tobacco and other supplies. A steel mirror is bolted to the face of the locker. I halt before it and look at my hair. It's nearly grown back. I'm glad I'm not the freak I was after I first came here, hair clipped short, my head looking like an egg. I wouldn't want Joyce to see me like that.

Saturday morning. The pass comes from the visiting room. Pete signals me. I slip into my uniform and scoot for the front gates. There are only two other visitors in the room, and the turnkey motions me right in. The same guard who supervised the visit with my mother sits at lazy inattention. He initials my pass, arranges chairs, and waits for my visitor. I squirm on the edge of my chair.

Then the gates rattle and clang, and Joyce is walking through the door of the visiting room. She is a mist of dark hair and white dress and graceful motion.

I clutch her to me, hold her tight, close my eyes.

She murmurs, "Darling, darling."

I whisper, "It's been so long."

The perfume of her hair is intoxicating. My head feels giddy, and I want only to stand here with her in my arms, motionless.

"I've missed you so terribly."—Joyce.

I hold her face in my hands, look long at it, then kiss her gently. Yes, her lips are even softer than I'd dreamed. She tries to smile, but her eyes are clouded with unhappy mists.

The guard says, "You'll both have to sit down now."

I slump to my chair and look at Joyce. I can't tear my eyes from her face. I see her as though she is some beautiful picture dimly outlined through a foggy veil. . . . She wipes her eyes. The picture clears. There are the smile, the white teeth, the crown of dark hair, the smooth, soft skin, that tantalize me during every hour, awake or asleep.

She says, "Frank, dear," and shakes her head.

"Don't feel bad, Joyce. I think I'm going to get a break now."

"Have you heard something?"

I nod. "Nothing definite, though it looks good. . . .

But let's not waste time talking about that. I wrote you a special letter last night."

Her face lights. "But what is it?"

"Just a new angle I figured out . . ." I glance at the guard, who is, as usual, staring sadly at his shoes. My eyes describe a quick danger signal to Joyce. Her mouth quivers . . . "It's all in the letter," I add. "And I tried to make the letter the same sort we used to write so long ago when we were in high school. Remember?"

Her face lights imperceptibly, like the brief glow of a firefly. She says slowly, "Oh, yes," and I know that she understands.

I switch to a less dangerous topic.

"My mother said," I begin, "that they'd found Limpy in California."

"Well, they haven't really found him yet, but Bill and Lew got hold of a man that said he was sure Limpy'd suddenly acquired a lot of money just after your trouble started, and that as far as he remembered Limpy left for California right after that."

"Who's the A. P. fellow that's looking it up?"

"Ray Pick—remember him? He was a photographer."

"Has he got anything to work on?"

"Limpy's supposed to have gone to Los Angeles. . . . If he's still there, or has been there, Ray'll find him. Then Bill or Joe will go out to the coast and see what they can get out of him."

"How does the lawsuit business against the paper look?"

"Not very well. They're desperate to get you out right away, before the cases go to trial."

I shake my head. "If they lose those suits and have to pay them, it may cause the sheet to fold."

I take Joyce's hand and hold it to my cheek. Her palm is soft and warm, and I think of the thousands of times I've wished that hand could have been on my forehead, dissolving my fears and despairs. . . . She speaks in a low tone of all her hopes for our future. Despite all past adversity, she still believes that I'll be free in only a short time—that the paper will be able to work a miracle.

I say, "About that business of the paper changing policy and supporting the administration to help me— nothing doing."

She smiles quizzically. "Yes, so we learned. Joe felt the Governor out on it, and they don't even want our support. They feel that we want to get back aboard the bandwagon, now that the fight is over and our side lost."

I curse to myself. "Why in the world did Joe lay himself open like that? Every other sheet in the city'll be laughing at him now. . . . I wouldn't have gone for a release under those conditions."

Joyce shakes her head. "Well, it's too late now. . . . But it was a nice gesture on Joe's part."

Then I feel the officer's hand touch my knee.

"Half hour's up." he says.

"Already?" I gasp. It seems as if Joyce had arrived only a moment ago. Yet, this has been a happy visit; there has been almost none of the sorrow that marked the visit with my mother. But Joyce is young, and she cannot be expected to be so deeply touched by seeing me here as my mother, who is old. Nor can Joyce be hurt by the disgrace of my imprisonment. Youth is like a coat of armor against some of the tragedy that touches the world.

I hold Joyce in my arms, take a last long look at her face.

"I'll see you once a month," she promises—"every time I'm allowed to come down here."

"Please write often."

"I will—every night."

"And keep me informed. Let me know when anything new turns up."

"I will. And I'll be thinking of you every moment."

I kiss her. Now again my heart is beating fast and my mind is a blur of swirling thoughts of her. She is so close—the sound of her voice, the warmth of her face, memory of happy hours together—all rush over me in a wave.

She whispers, "Good-by, dearest."

I take enormous strides all the way back to the twine plant, and tear into my work with a vengeance. Fargo Red sneaks up beside me and, when Pete isn't looking, mutters, "You gone nuts, you crazy son-of-a-bitch?"

By afternoon, rain has started to fall, and we must

take our half-holiday in the corridor of the cell halls. As soon as we break ranks, I happily slam Red on the back. The hairy man shakes me off, gets me over against the window sill and starts to throttle me.

"Now I know you're nuts," he growls. "What the hell happened this morning?"

"My girl was here to see me, you big ape. Isn't that a reason to feel good?"

"Girl!" snorts Red, releasing me. "I've had a million of 'em, but you don't see me running around like a Zulu with a hot iron in his mitts."

Lassiter and Mueller join us.

"Sure," says Lassiter. "One good look at a girl and an Eskimo pie'd kill you."

Red lines his jaws with snuff. "Laugh all y' want, baby. But I've had my moments."

I say, "Big stuff, hey, Red?"

"Sure. There was that time I was walking along Two Street in Mountain City, wondering where I was gonna sleep, when a bim puts the arm on me. 'C'mon up t' my room,' she says, 'an' I'll take care of you.' Just like that. 'I ain't got no dough,' I says. So she says, 'You don't need no dough with me,' she says. 'I like your looks,' she says." Red grins. "It's always been like that with me an' women. I coulda had a thousand of 'em."

"Well, go on," prompts Lassiter. "What happened then?"

"So we flag up to her room—she's got a flea bag on Eleventh Avenue, if y' know where that is. A dump district right near the market. I told her I wouldn't stay there because I hadda get out an' hustle up a pair of shoes fer myself. So she says, 'Stick around, Toots; I'll buy you a pair of shoes in the morning.' "

Red's jaws work, and he grimaces and shakes his head.

I ask, "Did you let her buy you the shoes?"

"Hell, no!" he snorts. "I wouldn't trust no woman like that. I've lost too much giving credit. I made her gimme the dough right then and there. . . . An' then I beat it out an' got a pint. . . . I bet she's still waiting."

Lassiter and I howl. Red grins conceitedly. "Women," he adds, "are always wantin' t' buy me something."

Mueller says nothing—merely stares out the window at the rain slanting down across the prison yard.

Lassiter says, "Cheer up, pal. The board'll meet before so very long, and then we'll both be out of here."

"Maybe you will," glooms Mueller, "but I won't."

"Yes, you will. And then you're coming right home with me for a nice long rest. Get this joint out of your bones and then try to make a new start."

"Not me, Lassiter. Whether I get out or not, I've got a date to keep."

"Quit thinking about Pete."

Mueller growls, "I've got a date with Pete, and I'm gonna keep it either in here or out." His lips close tightly; his eyes smolder. "That dirty little pup. I'd rather get him and make sure he's dead than have somebody give me the keys to this joint. I'd rather do the job on the outside, but if he keeps riding us, I'll tangle with him right in here."

"Forget about it, Mueller," says Lassiter softly. "You know we're your pals, and you know we wouldn't give you a bum steer. Lay off brooding over that guy. It's harder to control than religion in a joint like this." He slaps Mueller's arm. "All this stuff of planning what you're going to do to somebody is just in the head. It's a condition that comes over you because you're in prison and have no outlet for your emotions. After you're outside, you won't even think of Pete."

Mueller stares hard at us. "That's what you think. But I've been in plenty of prisons before. I know."

"But look how he rides Frank and me. And Red— good Lord, he's kept Red here over seven years. But we don't let it get us down. It'll all be over some day."

"Yes," spits Mueller. "It'll be over for me when I'm dead. But I'm not leaving this earth without taking Pete with me. I'm in here on a bum rap, and somebody's going to pay for it." He pauses a moment, and then, "You don't know anything about doing time. You and Ross were never locked up before. Pete's taking advantage of it to make you more miserable. And he hates you because you're smarter than he is and have been around some. Me—he hates me be- cause he knows I hate him. That goes for Red too. And he ain't gonna get away with it any more, once

that pardon board meets. . . . I see Pete every place.
I dream about him. . . . Maybe I'm blowing my top;
maybe I'm going stir-nuts. I guess I've done too
much time as it is, without doing this bum rap too. . . ."
He looks at Red. "Do you think I'm going nuts?"

Lassiter and I exchange glances.

Red snorts, "Hell no. I been talkin' t' myself fer
years. I wake up when the bell rings, an' it's fifteen
minutes after I get up before I know whether I'm
afoot or horseback. No kiddin'—I sometimes keep
right on dreamin' fer two or three minutes after I'm
outta bed. . . . An' I imagine the damnedest things.
Take this morning. I musta been dreamin' pretty
hard because after the bell rang I jest laid there fer
quite a while tryin' t' figure out where I was—me,
that's been here over seven years! I thought fer a
minute I'd been on a drunk last night an' got throwed
in the hokey-pokey."

"Sure, it's the same with all of us," says Lassiter.
"Just take it easy for a little while, Mueller; we'll be
out of here before you know it. And then you won't
be even thinking about Pete any more."

Mueller's face sags. "You mean you think we'll
both really get a break? I can't believe it. My luck
couldn't stand it. . . . You may get out, but my past
record'll keep me here till I do it all and go out the back
gate. I haven't got any money or friends, and from
the looks of things, that pardon board isn't operated
on a credit basis."

"You' damn right," growls Red. "Some of the stuff the board pulls stinks out loud. Look at that Gleason case. Seven years ago, Joe and Louie Gleason come down here with straight life raps—no chance of a parole, ever. They put some guy on the spot in an alky war. They do three years, then Louie Gleason says he done the shooting an' his brother didn't have nothin' t' do with it. So the pardon board cuts Joe's sentence t' thirty years. The next month the parole board turns him out. Then, after Louie's admitted he done the killing, the pardon board cuts his sentence to thirty years, an' damn if the parole board doesn't turn him out too. I hear it cost the Gleasons thirty grand. . . . An' the board won't do a thing fer people like Dale. He gets the book fer knockin' down a whore that was drunk an' tryin' t' kick him where it does the least good. An accident. She hit her head on a steam pipe an' died a few days later. But the pardon board wouldn't spit on Dale if he was burnin'. He ain't got no dough or connections. An' me—I got in over seven years fer stealin' a tire, but will they gimme a break? Hell no. . . . Somebody oughta start something around here. Things is goin' too good. Mebbe if they had a damn good riot they wouldn't be so anxious t' keep us here when we shoulda been out years ago. . . . Kill off a few of these dirty screws an' bloody up the cell halls an' set fire t' the shops. That'd give 'em something t' think about. . . ."

"You'd better keep your mouth shut about anything like that, Red," says Lassiter. "Just let the deputy or the warden get an idea you're agitating, and you'll be lucky if you ever get out of the hole."

"Nuts!" snorts Red. "I ain't a-scared of that hole. I been in it so much I don't feel at home in my cell no more."

"Just the same," warns Lassiter, "if I were you——" He breaks off and doubles over in pain.

Mueller and I catch him.

"What's the matter?" asks Mueller tenderly. "Got a cramp, pal?"

Lassiter gasps and contorts his face. A crowd of inmates quickly gathers, but several officers investigate the ganging up. I see that among the men whom the officers dispersed is Carlisle. He honors me with his choicest sneer.

Lassiter has difficulty breathing. We are about to try to be of some help, but just then the bell rings, and the holiday is over. Two officers shuffle down the corridor with Lassiter sagging between them.

We fall into line. Silence closes down. All the inmates crane their necks at the trio passing into the rotunda, then eye each other half defiantly, half fearfully. Their glances seem to say, "Well, it wasn't me. . . . But maybe I'm next."

I sit on my cot and think about Lassiter. Then, after a long time, footsteps sound on the gallery, and the drop bar slams back. Lassiter passes my cell, moving slowly and painfully, and halts next door, in front of his own. He smiles, but is very pale. I wish to talk with him but don't dare, for if the screw coming down to unlock his cell door isn't Mac, I'll get thrown in the hole if I'm caught talking from my cell.

Lassiter whispers, "I'm feeling better now."

Then Mac comes down the gallery and unlocks Lassiter's cell door.

"What was it, Mac?" I ask.

"Just a crick in the back, according to what the head nurse told him," answers Mac.

"That bastard," whispers Mueller, from the cell on my other side.   "Who can believe him?"

"He's a dirty son, all right," agrees Mac.

11

I GET a call to the deputy warden's office. Armstrong, the deputy, says, "This is Ross, Mr. Coping." A man in a gray business suit shakes hands with me.

"I'm district attorney of Stony Point county," says Coping. "I want to ask you a few questions concerning the Ludke killing."

I say, "Shoot."

"Now, you're positive that the knife deputy Armstrong showed you is the one you saw Stacey practicing with?"

"Yes."

"Describe what you saw in the twine shop the day Stacey was practicing."

I give him the details.

"Why didn't you come out with this information before?" he asks.

"I was afraid. Ludke was killed, you know. I don't want the same thing to happen to me."

Coping nods. "Now, what makes you so sure Stacey threw the knife?"

"He was sitting right across from Ludke during the show. And he used to be a knife-thrower with a circus or a carnival. . . . Up in the shop, he was throwing the knife and hitting the same spot every time, even with his eyes closed."

120

"Not that we don't believe he's the guilty party," says Coping, "but we'll have to do more than guess when we take him down for trial. . . . Didn't he ever make any threats?"

"Not outright. Stacey isn't the type of man to talk about what he's going to do. All I know is that the knife that was found in Ludke was owned by Stacey, and that Ludke had ratted on Stacey, giving Stacey a motive for the killing."

"Well," says Coping, "it isn't a very strong case. There's no telling what a jury'll do when Stacey's attorney starts pounding on the fact that there were over three thousand inmates in the chapel, each of whom might have had a reason to kill Ludke. But we'll try it."

"When do I have to go to court?" I ask.

"Next Friday. Stacey's already been indicted by the grand jury."

I leave the deputy's office and head back to the shop. . . . Next Friday. That will be four days away.

Red seems fidgety when I get on my overalls and report back to the breaker. Mueller, who is working with us now that Stacey's gone, is piling bales at the machine. Red stoops from sight and motions for me.

"So you been holding out on your pal, hey, you damn jail-breaker?" he says.

"What're you trying to do, kid somebody?"

"Nuts! I just been talking t' Mose. Stacey sent out word you was helping him to make a break." Red's eyes are filled with admiration. "I never thought it of you, kid. You're sure okay."

He shakes my hand. I break down and confess. "Keep your mouth shut, you big gorilla, or I won't tell you what happens in the courtroom."

"How's he gonna make out?"

"I don't know. No, honest, Red, I don't. He wouldn't tell me. But he's sure it'll work. And after he's out, he's going to run down the birds that framed me and somehow turn them in with full confessions."

"Liable to get caught himself, trying a thing like that."

"Don't worry. A guy as smart as Stacey isn't going to be caught very easy."

"I wonder," says Red, "is they any chance fer me to ace in on this thing. I could tell the deputy I know something about it too, an' then mebbe I'd get a chance t' go to court an' could lam with Stacey."

"No chance. Stacey told me only one man could make it the way he's going."

"Pretty damn swell. An' here all the time I thought you was just a dumb newspaper guy!"

Mueller shuts down the machine, walks back to the oil tank, and hisses. Pete is looking in our direction. Red and I cautiously rise.

Now that Stacey has sent word out to the good heads, I'm in double danger. If word reaches the deputy, Stacey's chances are gone, and I'm as good as in the hole right then. Stacey shouldn't have taken the chance, for if a rat should accidentally get wind of this, both Stacey's and my chance at freedom will be gone. They'll take an army down to the county seat with Stacey and may even keep the handcuffs on him while he's in court—an unheard-of thing in this state. . . . But Stacey probably figured that if he didn't send out word clearing me, one of his friends might blow his top over my apparently having turned rat and kill me. Now the good heads at least will know that my snitching was for a purpose other than my own good. All Stacey and I can do between now and the date of his hearing is hope that none of the good heads talk this over within earshot of Carlisle.

Mueller, too, has been informed, for he grins as Red starts up the machine. "Nice work, Frank. I had a hunch you and Stacey were pulling something when you went over to the deputy's just before Stacey went to the hole."

He takes my arm in a grip of steel and gives it a squeeze.

"Make more room around here, hey?" he says. "We need it, boy. The cons are starting to hang out the windows, the joint's so crowded."

And he is certainly right about the crowded condition of the cell halls. This condition alone has the inmates on edge and makes it all the harder to do time in here. As Red said in the cell hall Saturday, and as many inmates have said for a long time, the crowded condition is going to lead to a riot unless some steps are taken so the men will have a little more privacy. About two hundred inmates sleep on cots in the north cell hall and about the same number in the south block. Added to these cot-dwellers are several hundred in the school rooms and fifty or sixty in the night crew's cell hall. School has had to discontinue because of the congestion. The cot-dwellers have no privacy whatsoever, sleeping about four feet from each other; and the men in the cells on the ground floor—the longtimers—just about go crazy having to watch the inmates on the cots in front of them.

Lassiter, who now must work on the same machine with Carlisle, raises his hand. After a long wait, Pete nods. Lassiter crosses the shop to Pete's stand and shouts something at the guard. Pete shakes his head. Lassiter holds his back and talks some more. Pete's face darkens, and he yells at Lassiter, waving his arms violently. Lassiter returns to his machine. His face is white; he looks like death.

Mueller growls, "Lassiter looks sick. If I thought he was, and Pete wouldn't let him go to the hospital——"

Just then Deputy Armstrong makes the rounds of the shops and stops in our doorway. Without permission, Lassiter leaves his machine and goes to the deputy. Armstrong nods his head and motions Pete an okay. Lassiter goes behind the clothes rack and dons his uniform. Pete scribbles a pass and throws it at Lassiter, screaming some invective the while. Lassiter seems too sick to understand or care what Pete is yelling. He turns and, walking slowly, leaves the shop.

Just before noon, he returns, still looking very sick and wan and tired. At noon I sit beside him in the dining hall. As soon as the bell rings, I ask him what was wrong.

"It's that crick in my back again. Started again last night. Can't imagine what causes it. Bad headache with it too."

"What'd they say at the hospital?"

"The head nurse looked me over and gave me some C-C pills. I couldn't see the doctor. The nurse said it wasn't anything—just a crick."

"Dirty bastard," growls Mueller, who sits on the other side of Lassiter. "He couldn't open a boil, and they let him handle sick men. . . . Was that all they did for you?"

"The nurse let me lie down in the dressing room for a while. I wanted him to put the sun-lamp on my back, but he wouldn't do it."

"Does it still hurt you, kid?" asks Mueller tenderly.

"Yes, some. Hard to breathe, especially when I stand up. Feels like a knife sticking in my back."

"Go on back to the hospital after lunch. Raise hell with them if they won't give you any treatment. Send for the warden."

Lassiter smiles wanly. "Send for the warden? Gosh, I've never seen the guy but twice since I've been here, let alone talked with him. And I asked for an interview about ten times."

"Well, then," I say, "send for the deputy. He's a square-shooter. Tell him how they're treating you

and he'll give you a break.   He's trying to keep everything here on the level, but he hasn't a chance if he
doesn't know what's going on."

"I'd better not.   Pete's plenty sore now because I
went over his head this morning.   I'll ask Pete for another pass this afternoon.   I don't think he'd have the
nerve to turn me down, now that the deputy knows."

"The hell with Pete," growls Mueller.   "You're a
sick man—white as a ghost.   Don't depend on Pete
to help you."

"Oh, he'll let me go up to the hospital all right, now.
If I don't feel better, I'll get a pass right after lunch."
He pauses, then says, "The pardon board meets in a
few months, and my attorney thinks I'm going to get
out. . . . God, wouldn't it be tough to kick off just
about the time my pardon papers were being sent down
here?"

"Don't worry, Lassiter," I say.   "You'll be eating
Christmas dinner with your wife and kids.   And
maybe Mueller will too. . . . Men die in here, all
right—plenty of them.   But not us.   We'll pull
through all right."

"I don't know.   I feel pretty tough," says Lassiter.
"Kind of dazed, as though I'm just floating around
in space."

We march back to the shop.   As we are changing
our clothes, Lassiter asks Pete for a pass.   Pete roars,
"Y' ain't gittin' away with no more of that gold-
brickin'!   Y' sneaked up t' the deputy an' pulled the
wool over his eyes this morning, but y' ain't puttin'

nothin' over on me. . . . G'wan. Git that uniform off an' git into them overalls."

Lassiter says, "But I can't. I'm so weak I can hardly stand up. I can't breathe, and ——"

"Git them clothes off!" screams Pete. He shoves Lassiter with his cane. Lassiter trips over the clothes rack, attempts to catch himself, and falls across an iron drawbar. There is a snap as the bar hits his back.

Pete, looking frightened, kneels and examines Lassiter. He tells the Wolf and Carlisle to help Lassiter to the hospital and keep their mouths shut about how Lassiter was hurt. The pair nods and hustles Lassiter away.

12

SILENTLY we file to our positions and start the machine. But our minds are crowded with thoughts of Lassiter and the pain written on his face when he was pushed by Pete. Yet we dare not speak of it, for Pete is on a rampage following his trouble with Lassiter, and if we talk, we're sure to go to court. All we can do is perform our work and cast occasional sick glances at each other and shake our heads.

The Wolf and Carlisle return from the hospital and hold a long conversation with Pete. At its conclusion, Pete looks anything but pleased. He motions the pair to their work, and fixes our machine with a murderous glare. At that moment, Red is trying to get Mueller to bend down behind the machine and talk, but I warn them in time.

Carlisle joins the Wolf, who has taken Lassiter's place at Carlisle's machine. The pair eye each other in pleased manner, as though something good has just happened to them.

Red takes a chance and growls, "A fine pair of bastards they make. Happy because Lassiter's in the hospital!"

"Yes," snarls Mueller, taking no precautions whatsoever, "and that Wolf son-of-a-bitch is getting to be just as big a rat as Carlisle."

128

I take a hasty look at Pete's desk, but luckily he's not looking our way, but rather is now beaming on Carlisle and the Wolf.   Then he turns to watch us, and senses our rebellion, and climbs down from his raised stand.

At this moment, the twine fiber starts to wind around the roller of our machine.   Red shuts it off, and we drop to our knees and start to pick at the tightly wound fiber with sharp little bale knives.   Red crawls under the machine and starts cleaning the far side of the roller with his knife.   He motions as if he'd like to jab it in Pete's belly.

Pete wheezes around the front end of the breaker. He seems disgruntled further than usual at finding us busily occupied and not talking or loafing on the job. He halts beside Mueller and stands tapping his cane against the floor.   He has a mania for tapping. Whether he is on his stand or touring the shop, he continually taps with his cane, his foot, his pencil or his fingers.   And when he is aroused, the tapping mounts to a frenzied tattoo.

"Clean that out good," he grunts.   "None of your shiftlessness for once."

He is continually issuing needless orders, possibly realizing how much they enrage us.   The fact that we are cleaning out the fiber as fast as we possibly can means nothing to Pete.   He pays no heed whatsoever to the other nine machines in the shop.   Their operators are not required to do any cleaning or repairing; the oiler and the shop mechanic attend to everything.

Yet Pete demands that our machine be perpetually
spotless, even when it is running and great choking
clouds of dust rise from the dry fiber.   Every night he
inspects the breaker, usually after we are cleaned up
and ready to go to the dining hall for supper.   He de-
lights in making us change clothes and reclean the
machine.   It is not that he cares whether or not the
shop equipment is dirty; for he himself is habitually
filthy, and the other nine machines are caked with
layers of oil and dust.   He is merely unhappy unless
he is finding fault with us and making our lives just a
little more miserable. . . . He is even worse since
Mueller is now in this crew.

At last we get all the fiber cleaned away.   Pete
stoops, like a caricature of a baby hippopotamus, and
peers at the roller.

"What the hell's the matter with you?" he cries.
"Tryin' t' put somethin' over on me?   Lookit that
piece of machinery!   Covered thick with dust.   Clean
it off."   He pokes his cane into the breaker and rubs
the offending part.   "An' don't lemme catch yuh
tryin' nothin' like that again."

"We can't get that off," I try to explain.   "The
night crew shellacked the roller last night and ran the
breaker while the stuff was still wet.   That dust is
stuck in it."

"Yeah," Red drawls from beneath the machine.
"That's right.   The dust's stuck in it."

"Aha!" cries Pete.   "You two been talkin' again,
hey?"

"We haven't said a word."

"Then how the hell yuh both know about this roller
if yuh didn't tell each other?"

"I can see, can't I?"

"No yuh can't see. An' yuh don't know enough t'
know that's shellac. Neither one of yuh. Somebody
told yuh. I'm too smart fer you guys. I kin outwit
yuh, that's what's the matter with yuh."

Red crawls from beneath the machine. Mueller,
who has stood near by and said nothing, opens up.

"They haven't said a word."

"Shut your mouth! Who the hell's talkin' t' you!"

Red demands belligerently, " 'Smatter? Can't a
guy notice a little shellac without talkin'?"

"Who ast you t' put your oar in this? Git back
there an' git t' work! G'wan! Git the hell under that
machine an' scrape off that shellac!" Red crawls back,
white with rage. Pete swings on Mueller and me.
"A couple of wise guys! You mighta been lucky on
the outside, but I'm the boss an' the smart guy in here.
I know all the answers, an' yuh don't git by on luck
with me."

He waddles away, pounding the floor with his cane,
and rolling back his eyeballs until only the whites show.
Mueller's face is a picture of murderous rage. His
eyes flash and his lips and throat twitch. But he
kneels and commences to scrape at the shellac with a
bale knife.

In a few minutes, the deputy's runner enters the
shop and hands three passes to Pete. I glance at the

clock. **One thirty.** Time for court. And three men from our shop are going to lose their privileges.

We aren't kept long in suspense. Pete's finger levels first at Mueller, then at Red, then at me.

We change our clothes and line up in front of Pete's stand. Red demands, "What's the rap this time?"

"You'll damn soon find out," squeals Pete. "I'll show you guys you ain't in no county jail or workhouse now. You're in the stir, by Jesus!"

"Naw," drawls Red. "Not really! An' here I been thinkin' all the time I was workin' in a ladies' riding academy."

"What's that!" screams Pete, beating the floor of the stand with his cane. "Was you givin' me any lip?"

"Who, me? I ain't said a word."

"What'd he say, Mueller?"

"What am I supposed to be—the new rat around here?"

"What!"

"I said he didn't say a word."

"By Christ, I'm gonna have all of yuh in that hole, an' once I put yuh there again, yuh'll do the book in there before yuh git out." He flings passes at us. "Yuh'll toe the mark in my shop, an' no back talk. If I thought you guys was givin' me any lip then—— G'wan! Git the hell outta here! Git over there t' court. One more word outta any of you, an' I'll stand yuh up against that wall"—the procedure when an inmate waits to be taken to the hole.

We file down the stairs, across the yard, and into the anteroom of the deputy's office. The guard who is always on duty during the court time lines us up with about twenty other sad-eyed inmates. The guard is Mad Dog Mooney. He opens the door of the deputy's private office, lets out an inmate, and shoves the next in line forward. We hear the deputy's barking voice. The inmates shuffle their feet woefully and look at their shoes. The line moves steadily ahead. One man is led from the deputy's office by an assistant and taken into the solitary. . . .

And then I am next. I pass through the door and halt beside Armstrong's desk. He does not look up at me—merely reads the report.

"Ross, you're reported for talking to Mueller."

"I didn't talk. It's a bum rap."

"Mean to call the officer a liar!"

"Can't he ever make a mistake?"

"You're going to mistake yourself right into the hole. . . . Get out of here."

I get out of there. The captain of the solitary sits at his desk and initials my pass. Red enters the deputy's office. I return to the shop.

Mueller and Red return shortly after me. Small worry now whether Pete sees us talking. In fact the fat little guard, once he has sneered at us, completely ignores us. I look around. Carlisle is working at his machine, but the Wolf is not beside him. Instead, he has Cooper working with him. And I am glad of that, for Cooper is in the prison band, and goes out for practice three mornings a week, leaving his partner to do the work alone.

Mueller, Red and I crouch behind the breaker.

"How d'yuh like that for a stinking, foul, bum rap?" demands Red. "Pete sent me to court for talking to Carlisle this morning, and I wouldn't even look at the dirty rat bastard."

"What'd he get you for?" I ask Mueller—"talking to me this morning?"

"Yeah. But give him enough rope and he'll hang himself. I can't stand much more of this."

"What's become of the Wolf?" I ask. "He wasn't at his machine when I got back, and Pete's already got Cooper helping our rat friend."

"There's another thing," says Red. "All you got to be around here is a wrong guy and you'll get a good job. Now they've got that dirty Wolf on the runner's job in the cell hall. He can go any place he wants, and eats on the special table."

"How do you know?" asks Mueller.

"He came in the deputy's office just as I came out from court. I heard Captain Temple telling him what to do."

"If that don't beat all hell," mutters Mueller. "Not only a dirty swive on the outside, but a rat in here, and he gets a job like that. How'd you suppose he worked it?"

I hazard, "I'll bet Pete had something to do with it. The Wolf's covering up for him on Lassiter, you know."

"Just watch," says Mueller. "If that's the case, Carlisle'll be a walking boss around here before you know it. Then we'll really do some tough time."

"Son-of-a-bitch," growls Red. "I'm gonna talk to Mose."

I start the breaker, and Mueller stands by, ready to drag out and weigh the bales as fast as I complete them. Red holds his hand aloft. I complete two bales—ten minutes—before Pete condescends to nod. Red vanishes behind the swinging door of the latrine. In a moment I can see him talking with Mose through the open space at the bottom.

By the time Red returns, the machine has broken down—it is twenty-five years old and breaks down on an average of three times each day. Were it not for the breakdowns, we'd have to work steadily all day; whereas Pete permits the other operators to shut down for the day over an hour and a half before us. . . . The break is a major one, thank God, and the mechanic will, for once, have to repair it himself. While he and his helper are making the repairs, Mueller, Red and I crouch from sight behind the machine.

"The scurvy louse," Red snarls at Mueller. "Pete told Mose, when he sent him over to the deputy's office with them reports, that he's gonna ride you right into the nuthouse. . . . He's really gunning fer you now, and no fooling. Carlisle and the Wolf told him you hated the guts of all screws and Pete's guts in particular. He's wild."

Mueller licks his lips and nods thoughtfully.

Red continues, "And Carlisle told him I was making signs this morning and you and Ross were talking. . . . What I wouldn't like to do to that rat. Too bad Stacey didn't bump him too."

I ask, "You mean Carlisle engineered the whole deal and Pete went for it?"

"Hell, yes. Besides, Carlisle knows you got a birthday Sunday, and he couldn't bear t' think of you enjoying the pitcher show on your birthday."

Mac halts in front of my cell and eyes me soberly.

"Lassiter's gone out," he says.

"No!" I jump up from my chair and experience the first real joy I've known since I came to Stony Point. "Honest to God, Mac?"

"Yeah, they shipped him home to his wife and kids."

"Jesus! Home! I'll bet he isn't even sick any more."

"No, sickness won't be bothering Lassiter now."

Mac's face is deadly serious. He particularly likes Lassiter and has gone out of his way many times to help him. Yet he doesn't seem happy over Lassiter's release. . . . A chill touches me.

"Why?" I ask. "Everything's okay, isn't it?"

"Sure, if you look at it the right way, everything's swell. He's gone out, hasn't he? He's on his way home." He pauses and then clips off short, biting sentences. "He went out the back gate. In a hearse. He's dead."

I catch at the bars, press close and search his face. "You don't really mean it, Mac. You're kidding."

But I know from his face that my words are idle.

"God almighty, Mac. It can't be true. I ate with him this noon. He's up for a pardon. He worked——" I cease my aimless ranting. My knees are like water. I collapse on the chair. . . . "What was it?"

"I couldn't find out for sure, but the night captain said he heard it was either spinal meningitis or a broken back or both."

"Pete pushed him today, and he fell on his back. It hurt him so bad he passed out."

"If it's a broken back, they'll cover it up. I saw plenty of stuff like this when I was in the army during the war. Christ, how they used to kill them off!"

I start muttering to myself.

"Don't let it get you down, Ross," says Mac. "You'll blow your top if you harp on it."

Mac stops at Mueller's cell, and I hear them whispering. I stare frozenly at the floor. . . . Many inmates have died since I was sentenced to prison, but Lassiter's death is the first to touch me directly—to take something out of my own life. For Lassiter was my friend. I had always believed that some day we'd all be free to leave our unhappiness here with the gray walls and the wasted portions of our lives—to forget all that we have endured. But to live through years of silence and misery, to accept discouragements and rebuffs, to withstand abuse and humiliations, to drag ourselves through an existence that is worse than death, buoyed only by the hope that the future might hold something fine in store for us, and then to die, here in prison, without even a last glimpse of the outside world—— God, oh, God!

Mueller's whispers become louder and hoarser. Mac tries to quiet him. And then it happens.

Mueller's tin cup crashes to the floor. "God damn their dirty souls to hell! They've killed my pal! But I'll get them! I'll kill the sons-a-bitches that croaked my pal!"

As the lights go out, an hour later, Mueller is sobbing angrily, and Mac, thank God for a humanitarian, is coaxing him to undress and go to bed before the night captain comes around and hears him.

It is morning and we are in the shop. Mueller takes his place beside the machine. Pete watches him. Deliberately Mueller gazes across the shop and pretends to talk in sign language to someone at the far end. Pete gets out his report book and makes out a slip covering Mueller's infraction of the rules. He smiles to himself as he writes.

Mueller says, making no attempt to keep the motion of his lips from Pete, "Let him smile. I'll be laughing pretty quick."

Pete sees him talking and motions him to come to the stand. Mueller thumbs his nose at him. It's like lighting a fire-cracker under the fat little guard. He hops out of his chair, grabs his cane and starts screaming for Mueller to come to the platform. Mueller sits

down on a bale of manila, laughs crazily at Pete and
defiantly folds his arms. Pete scrambles down from
his stand and rushes at Mueller.

"Git up against that wall!" he screams. "You're
goin' t' the hole!" His face is purple with rage; he
stamps the floor with his cane. "Git up against that
wall! I'll bury you in that hole this time."

Mueller moves around in front of Pete, neatly trap-
ping him between the breaker and the wall.

"So you're the guy that wouldn't let my pal go to
the hospital," says Mueller slowly.

"I'll put yuh where he is if y' don't git outta my way
an' face that wall!"

Mueller's eyes are a pair of burning coals.

"And you're the guy," he continues, his voice rising,
"that knocked him down and busted his back."

"Git up against that wall!"

"And you're the guy that was gonna ride me into
the nuthouse."

"Carlisle, run fer the deputy!"

"Why, God damn you, you're the son-of-a-bitch that
killed my pal!"

Pete raises his cane. Mueller leans quickly to the
wall and snatches a bale hook from the rack. Pete,
suddenly panic-stricken, cuts at Mueller with his cane.
Mueller catches it across his shoulder, jerks it from
Pete's hand and flings it across the shop.

Pete retreats to the back of the breaker, where a wall
of raw twine fiber stops him. He attempts to scramble
over it. But Mueller swarms down on him. The

bale hook rips through the air, and the point plunges into Pete's neck. He collapses on the floor. His mouth slobbers bloodily.

Mueller cries, "This is for Lassiter!" The hook flashes down. Blood spurts. Pete claws with his hands; his fingers touch the holes in his neck. His lips move, and a great red bubble forms on his mouth and bursts with a tiny smack. I shut my eyes. "This is for Fargo Red!" *Thock!* "This is for Ross!" *Thock!* "This is for ——" *Thock! Thock! Thock!*

After an eternity the noises stop. Mueller stands astride Pete's body. Blood pours from the head and neck. The mouth sags open. The legs twitch. . . . My gaze fixes on Mueller, who caresses the hook and chuckles insanely.

"Life," I tell myself—"life in the hole. God, what a long, long time."

13

Now WE are entering upon a harsher, more closely guarded life—a life that threatens to become even more wretched than that we endured before Mueller killed Pete. Today in the dining hall we were all warned by Warden Tang himself—the first time he has ever entered the dining hall and spoken to the inmates. A tiny infraction of the prison's most obscure and ignored rules will bring instant and drastic punishment. To turn our heads while we are marching in line, to possess homemade snuff, to smile while at work or marching, to communicate by signs, to walk with our hands in our pockets, to make up our beds improperly—each and a thousand other infractions of the rules will be punished from now on with a long siege in solitary confinement.

We are under constant surveillance as a result of the killing. Our shop, which, because it is located on the third floor of the twine plant, was thought to be well out of the danger area, is now guarded by three officers. One occupies the stand, while the other two patrol the shop. Each changes places with the others every hour, forestalling any fraternizing of the guards with the inmates. The officers in the cell halls have been trebled. They pace the galleries and eye the cot-dwellers endlessly. . . . And the head guard in our shop

is now the cruel Mad Dog Mooney, who formerly
acted as Deputy Armstrong's assistant during court.
Some of us would almost rather have Pete back, for
Mooney has taken up where Pete left off.   Pete was
ignorant and abusive because he hadn't the intellect to
handle his authority.   Mooney is not only abusive and
cruel; he is also intelligent, and knows how best to
hurt those of us under him.

His first move was to make Carlisle a roving inspector—a walking boss, as Red put it.   Now Carlisle
tours the shop, ostensibly as an inspector of the twine,
but in reality to report any infractions of the rules he
sees.   No inmate, even if he is fortunate enough to
escape the eyes of Mooney and his assistants, Squires
and Lord, can hope to violate a rule and avoid the
darting glances of the prison's most notorious and best
guarded rat.   Each night he has instructions to turn
in slips to Mad Dog Mooney, naming every inmate he
saw commit an infraction of the rules during the day.
He follows up those instructions with a vengeance.
And I am a special target of his; I can take no
chances. . . . With not only the cunning of the dead
Pete, but also the cruelty and intelligence of Mooney,
Carlisle realizes how maddening it is to be reported by
a fellow inmate and made to suffer for an offense which
was not committed.

In every department of the prison, there is arising a
new tension—a feeling as though of slow strangula-
tion.   It catches at the throat and pounds in the
temples.   The slightest noises grate on the nerves like

wires probing into a deep and sensitive wound. At night, the dragging of a chair across a cell floor brings a storm of profane howls from a thousand throats. A cough, a moan, a sigh—and the air is filled with invective. Though the new rules have just gone into effect, the inmates already are showing signs of breaking and rising up against them.

Men have been at each other's throats on the slightest provocation today. A fancied hurt, a whispered word, a hostile glance—and down would go two inmates in a flurry of fists, blood on their hands and faces, murder in their hearts, panic in their minds, and long days of certain misery ahead. Fights broke out sporadically in the shops, in the cell halls, in the dining hall, and even while we marched to and from work. . . . If this keeps up, the solitary will soon be full.

Prison is a terrible place at its best. And now I must stay imprisoned in an institution which is at its worst. I fear that rioting and bloodshed lie ahead. The inmates, always overburdened with rules, will revolt against the unnecessarily stringent regulations which now govern their actions. Now, more than ever, I long to go home—to return to normal life. And now, more than ever, I must put my faith in Joyce and the boys on the paper. For I fear that my only hope of ever leaving this prison alive lies in them—and Stacey. How could I forget Stacey—when tomorrow is Friday, Stacey's day in court?

The pass comes from the deputy warden's office. Captain Temple rises from his desk as I enter the ante-room of Armstrong's office. The deputy is not in sight, but the captain of the solitary says, "All right, Ross. Go over and put those clothes on."

He leads me across the hall to the tailor shop and leaves me. The officer in charge indicates two sets of civilian clothes which are neatly spread out upon the long counter. A surprising thing happens. The guard details Dale, a lifer who is a friend of Red and who helped me get the lemon juice, to assist me in dressing.

I ask, "How come I rate a valet?"

The guard, a good-natured man who permits a certain amount of laxity in his department and who is therefore well liked, laughs.

"A lot of the men who are either going out or going to court ask that. Too bad you're not with the newspaper yet, for it would make a good item. Anyway, some of the men who leave this place have been here so long they can't remember how to put on a shirt with a stiff collar and can't tie a necktie. And most of the rest are so nervous and excited they can't dress alone even if they remember how."

He strolls to the back of the shop, toward the laundry and the entrance to the bathroom.

I whisper, "Well, I'll be damned. Is that right, Dale?"

"That's right. Need any help?"

"Hell, no!"

"Well, make off you do. I got something to tell you. We can chin while the bull thinks I'm putting on your collar and tie."

He is a venomous appearing little man, gray-haired and gray-faced from the years of imprisonment.

While he is pulling down the shades of the windows that open onto the hall, I look over my outfit. Black felt hat, coarse blue pin-striped suit, red string necktie, cheap white cotton shirt, stiff white collar of the Herbert Hoover vintage, high-top black shoes, and underclothes of heavy cotton. . . . I'll look like the great-grandfather of all the small-town undertakers since man started to die.

I work my way up to the shirt. Dale starts to help me.

"They're driving me nuts in here. This used to be a swell go, but since they tightened up we hardly dare make a move. Screw's on my tail all the time."

"It's the same in the shop," I whisper, keeping my eye peeled for the fat guard. "We get knocked off if we bat an eye."

"Pardon board turned me down last meeting," growls Dale. His eyes narrow. "If Stacey makes it, I got a good mind to crush out too."

"Don't try it. Too dangerous."

"Bull! I made it outta Chelan."

The door opens. Stacey and three guards enter. Stacey grunts as though in disgust, but when the screws look toward me, Stacey winks.

One guard growls, "Shut your trap and get those clothes on."

Dale whispers through his teeth, "The guy'd make a swell actor."

Stacey starts dressing. I don the coat, pick up the hat and cross the hall to the deputy's office. Already my heart is starting to thump at thought of what may lie ahead for Stacey—for both of us, for that matter.

Captain Temple marches me down the long hall to the front gates, where he leaves me with two guards between the third and fourth gates. . . . Just beyond them is the door which opens from the outside into the front office. Through that door I can see cars whizzing by, and people—free people—walking, and trees and green grass and the peaks of the mountains which rise far beyond the river. Soon I'll be outside these gates—a part of the free world where streets are long and wide and endless, and waters run deep and far, and a man is master of his own destiny. I'll be all that for a few minutes or hours today, and then I'll come back. I only wish I knew to what I'll return.

I stand silently between the guards—Hultman and Klein, who usually do duty in the mail room—and watch the world outside the office door. The guards say nothing. The minutes tick past. I ask the guards what is holding us up, for I want to get started and have the suspense over with. They do not reply.

Then I see the cause of the delay. Stacey comes down the hall shackled to two guards and led by the deputy himself. Another pair of officers falls in, making six guards and Deputy Armstrong as our body-guard. . . . Stacey has evidently had a hard time of it. In the darkness of the shaded tailor shop I didn't notice, but here in the light I see that his lips are swollen and one eye is slightly black. But he grins and winks again as they pass me.

I say to my guards, "Aren't taking much chance on losing either of us, are you?"

Neither answers.

The deputy leads his four officers and Stacey through the gates and out the front door. We wait a few moments; then Klein snaps handcuffs on me and man-acles himself to my wrist. The fourth gate swings back. We cross the lobby of the front office. Hult-man opens the door. I step outside the building—outside the walls—and breathe the air of free men for the first time in five long, dreary months.

Then my confinement and my sudden emergence into the land of the living make a kaleidoscope of my mind. Things happen suddenly; almost before they have regis-tered, another event crowds my former thoughts out of existence.

Klein and I stumble into the rear seat of the small sedan parked at the curb. The officer curses me for hurting his wrist. Hultman climbs behind the wheel. The starter whirs, the gears clash, and we move down the road toward the county seat, four miles away.

Klein pulls a blackjack from his pocket. "Don't try anything funny," he warns. "And just in case you can't take a hint, I've got a gun in my pocket." He is like a little boy who imagines himself very tough but backs his toughness up with the threat of a father or big brother, just in case—"Remember," he continues, "nobody's ever escaped from this joint or from the courtrooms. We've buried the ones that tried." He replaces the blackjack in his coat pocket.

Both he and Hultman are swollen fat with importance. Authority radiates from them. . . . They are taking an inmate of the state prison—a desperate criminal—to court as a witness in a murder trial. They are trusted employes of the state. They will bring the desperate criminal back to Stony Point with them, to serve out the remaining years he owes society. And all the world will fall at their feet and pay homage to their bravery. . . . Nuts!

The countryside whizzes by, a conglomeration of green grass and trees, cloudless blue skies, and buzzing traffic. To me, the momentum is terrific, but I glance over the front seat and see that the speedometer registers only thirty-five miles an hour. And to me that is saddening; for the slow marching, the slow passage of time, and the slow, methodical prison life have slowed my mind. I watch the mountains beyond the river, and after a mile or so, the road swings along the hillside, and I can look down upon the water. A cargo barge pushes against the current. A plume of steam blends with smoke from the stack. On the opposite shore, a train rushes into the west, its whistle echoing four long blasts of dying inflection.

Then we are crowding up the side of a hill, and veering away from the river, and swinging into the streets of the tiny county seat which stands above and away from the water's edge and dozes in the summer sunshine. . . . The tower of the three-story red brick courthouse glints faintly for a moment among the trees. We approach a cross-street, pause momentarily for a stop light, then halt before the entrance of the courthouse. Involuntarily I look up and see the windows of what must be the courtrooms on the third floor. Below them is a concrete drive. A long way down.

We enter the building. A single elevator creeps with us to the top floor. I shudder for Stacey. . . . Three flights up. A single elevator for an escape. Perhaps the elevator is even wired with signals, which warn the operator that an escape is being attempted, and he in turn blocks the stairway and cuts the current to the elevator until the police come. . . . Perhaps Stacey was having one of those gigantic pipe dreams, after all. . . . Poor Stacey.

A bailiff stops us at the door of the courtroom.

"Is this the last of them?" he asks.

Klein nods and removes the handcuffs. I am not surprised at this. Most judges object to having prisoners handcuffed in a court of justice. During the time I covered the police run for the *Record,* I never once saw a prisoner wearing cuffs in a courtroom.

The bailiff ushers us through the door. "Judge Crowder'll be here any minute. Court sits at nine."

He motions me across the room, inside the railed enclosure. "Go over there to that bench, on the other
side of the guy that's talking to his attorney."

I pass through the gate and cross the enclosure.
Stacey is deep in conversation with his lawyer—a
small, dark man who looks as if he might be made of
wire. A pair of guards stand outside the railing,
behind Stacey, and another pair eye him from near
the door of the courtroom. Hultman and Klein join
the deputy warden and then station themselves outside
the railing behind me. I turn to Armstrong.

"Is it okay if I sit by the window?"

He smiles his queer little half-smile and nods.

"Go ahead. You may not have the chance again
for a long while."

I sit on the edge of the bench, open my coat, and
lean my arm on the window sill. Across the courtroom, divided from me by the counselors' table, Stacey
is now silently listening to his lawyer. As usual, his
face is an expressionless mask. I wish that my com-
posure were all that his appears to be. Then he looks
up, sees me, and, after making certain that he will not
be observed, lets a faint grin touch the corners of his
mouth. Then he whispers something to the attorney.
After a moment, the lawyer rises and crosses the courtroom to me.

"I'm Charles Lockhart," he says, "Stacey's attorney.
Listen closely. If anyone asks you what I said now,
tell him that I merely asked you if you were certain
you could identify the knife, and that you said you

could." He glances around quickly, his keen little black eyes darting about like movable shoe buttons, waves to the deputy in offhand fashion and goes on hurriedly. "This is it. Everything's set. After he's gone, he'll keep in touch with you through me. That's all." He rises quickly.

The deputy comes up behind us.

"Just had a question to ask Ross," says Lockhart, and returns to Stacey's side.

"What'd he want with you?" growls the deputy.

I reply as the attorney instructed me.

"Did you tell him you could?"

"Yes, sir."

"Don't talk to him any more."

The deputy returns to his former position near the door. Hultman and Klein move back from the railing to the wall.

Then the door opens, and my heart does a flip-flop as Joyce and Bill Mason and Lew Keller enter. Behind them is another newshound—Jerry Poague, the *Record* cameraman. He has his box with him. It's all set there then. Joyce understood my meaning and read between the lines of the special letter. My mind tells me that it wishes this were over. What if Stacey lied and there is a shooting? What if Joyce gets hurt? I told her not to come, but should have known she would anyway. Now I could kill myself for writing that letter. It could have waited. The front-page beat wasn't worth it. But before the last thought has formed, I know that I'm lying to myself.

I start to stand up. Joyce waves at me. The deputy warden motions me to sit down. Joyce tackles Armstrong. She is very beautiful in her white dress and white hat and white shoes. Almost as beautiful as she is in winter, when her cheeks peep out from the folds of her fur coat and a breath of excitement emanates from every part of her. . . . Bill and Lew and Jerry join her in her argument with Deputy Armstrong. The deputy is adamant. He clamps his jaws shut tight and shakes his head in an emphatic no. The quartet bears down harder, emphasizing its pleas with much motion of the hands. Armstrong folds his arms, shakes his head in a final no, and looks over their heads. They give up in despair, turning to me and shrugging their shoulders.

All but Jerry. He talks earnestly with the deputy for a minute, then the first thing we know he's focusing his Graphic and shoving a bulb into the speedgun. Armstrong relaxes, smooths his coat, adjusts his tie, and tries to look like a deputy warden. Jerry pulls the slide, and the bulb flares. . . . In my mind I'm thinking, "Don't think you've been a fool, Armstrong, I've worked that old picture-in-the-paper-if-you'll-gimme-what-I-want gag on a hell of a lot of bigger men than you." Besides, why should the deputy warden squawk about newspaper people interviewing a prisoner? I've done it plenty of times, with permission, myself.

Joyce, Bill, Lew and Jerry fly back at Armstrong. He's looking half-pleased, half-angry for just having made himself look foolish.   I hear Jerry say, "I'll mail you the original and the cut as soon as we've run it, Mr. Armstrong."   Then the deputy nods his head.

But he adds, loud enough for me to hear, "Only for a minute, though."

The four come crowding around me, and I'm trying to kiss Joyce and shake the fellows' hands at the same time.   My kiss goes astray and lands somewhere near her nose.   But I rectify that.   She takes my face between the palms of her hands and pulls my head onto her shoulder and holds me like that for a moment. Then the fellows figure that that's enough of that and break it up.

"Good news, Frank," says Bill.   "We finally located that gimp-legged guy down in Los Angeles.   Ray Pick of the A.P. office found him, but the sheet's afraid to let him handle the questioning, so they're sending me down there by plane tonight."

Joyce hugs my arm.   "Maybe you'll be home before the month is over," she says.

They are all beaming, but I'm somewhat skeptical about Limpy.   "I don't know.   It's been a long time. And maybe he won't talk, anyway."

"He'll talk all right," promises Lew, balling his fist. "Bill'll see to that."

Joyce smiles and hugs my arm again.   Her trim little white hat is a perfect frame for the picture that is her face.   A flood of tenderness rushes over me.

I whisper, "If it could only come out that way."

"It will," says Lew. "I know it will. It has to. And when it does, won't it be sweet to think that those birds that engineered this will get life? It's plain first-degree murder on their part."

"I hope so, Lew. . . . But how come the whole bunch of you came down?"

"Holy smokes, guy," says Bill, waving his arms, "this's big stuff. Stacey's swell copy, and you're not so bad yourself."

"We're gonna hop on this and splash it all over the front page," supplements Lew.

"Look pretty," warns Jerry. The flash bulb blinds me. He reloads and shoots again. I grin. All I can see for a moment is a white sun floating around in a sea of black, and I feel sorry for all the poor dopes I've scared that way in the past. . . . Crazily, I remember the night I was making up the paper, and took a bulb holder into the composing room and banged the thing in Ray Hansen's face. He couldn't see to run his linotype machine for ten minutes.

Then Jerry heads for Stacey, who sits sullenly beside Lockhart. They both shake their heads, but the speedgun pops nevertheless . . . Jerry was always the best cameraman on the *Record's* staff. . . . During the next few minutes, as we talk, I unconsciously note the click of the electrically synchronized shutter and the flash of the bulbs as Jerry gets a complete picture record of the court scene.

"You fellows shouldn't have brought Joyce down," I say. "I was nuts when I wrote that letter."

"I told her to stay at the office, but she wouldn't," states Bill.

The guards are not near us, but stand back against the wall and watch Jerry, hoping, from the expressions on their faces, that he'll grab a shot of them. . . . I take a long chance.

"Listen, all of you. It's all set—due to bust in a few minutes. Tell Jerry to be ready. Take a look at his mouthpiece. Name's Lockhart. Big shot from the East, I guess. Do as he says if you ever hear from him. And if Stacey gets in touch with you, trust him—follow his instructions. This Limpy angle may peter out, and we'll have to fall back on Stacey."

Lew says, "Ixnay on the ackingcray. Joyce told us."

Joyce asks, "Will he really get out, Frank?"

"I'm beginning to believe it myself since I talked with Lockhart."

"And he'll help us—I just know he will."

"Sure he will, honey. It'll be duck soup for him, once he's out. Why, any gangster in the world would tell him anything he wanted to know. All he's got to do is keep asking till he finds the gangster that knows."

"Sounds screwy at first," Bill points out, "but after thinking it over, I really believe you've got something there."

"How do things look for the paper in the law suits?" I ask.

"Not so hot. They're about due to go to bat, and they're pretty worried. That's why Joe and Carney are sending me down there by plane tonight."

"Are you bearing up all right, Frank?" asks Joyce. "You're paler than when I saw you."

"Probably the excitement over today. . . . But I'm okay. It's just the uncertainty that gets me down. It's not much fun serving time for something I didn't do, and then not even being told whether I'll have to do one year or the whole twenty."

She holds my hand tight. "I know. I suffer with you too. . . . But it will soon be over. I can just feel it in my heart."

"How they treating you?" asks Bill.

"It's been pretty tough, but now it's worse since that guard got killed. The warden's clamped down hard."

"I wonder if we can help."

"No use. He hates the paper for the last write-up he got when he used state lumber and convict labor to do some building down by the river. . . . He's a vain old bird, you know."

"I'll spell the dirty old so-and-so's name wrong every time we use it," promises Bill.

The deputy moves over to the railing behind us. "All right. That'll be enough. Break it up now."

Joyce and the boys leave the railed enclosure and move to the back of the courtroom, where I see Bill whispering with Jerry the while Joyce and Lew talk with the deputy warden. . . . Jerry slaps a new bulb into his speedgun and stops down his lens.

District Attorney Coping enters and goes into an immediate huddle with Armstrong. . . . I stare out the window, across the roof tops, and watch the river,

a silver ribbon coiling through the emerald carpet of
grass and trees. A cargo barge hoots, and a smudge
of smoke trails down the river. . . . Already my imprisonment is falling from me like drops of rain from
an oiled surface. I marvel at this and wonder if the
past will dissolve itself as quickly when this phase of
my life is over. Sitting here in this courtroom, un-
shackled and in civilian clothes however poor, I feel as
though I am again a free man. The past—the yester-
days that have dragged past so endlessly—is already
becoming like something remembered from a bad
dream. Yet the odor of prison still clings to my nostrils. . . . I look around at Joyce and the boys. Joyce
smiles. Bill and Lew wear light gray summer clothes;
on a table are their panamas. Jerry is dressed in his
memorable white slacks and wine-colored, short-sleeved
sweater, open at the throat. . . . Armstrong motions
me to turn around.

My glance shifts to the cheap, coarse suit I wear.
It feels as though it is made of thistles. Sharp bits of
foreign matter stick through my heavy cotton underwear and keep my fingers busy. Stacey sees me
scratching, and flicks an imaginary speck from his
sleeve. I look out the window—down at the street
below me—to keep from laughing hysterically. . . .
His coolness is reassuring.

Then from my window I can see a large red sedan
slide to a halt in front of the courthouse. On the top
of the car, just above the rear cushion, is a splash of
white paint. . . . The driver, clad in a white Palm

Beach suit and a panama, climbs out of the car and starts across the walk. The face is familiar, and I try to get a better glimpse of it, but the man disappears beneath my line of vision. . . . And then suddenly I know. The man is Nate Garsky.

Now the courtroom is very warm. The trickle of summer morning air which comes through the open windows is like a hot blast. Perspiration floods down my face and over my body. The high collar chokes me. My nerves tighten, and I sit rigidly on the edge of the bench. . . . Stacey coughs and mops his face.

In a few moments the courtroom door opens a crack, and Garsky peers in. And during that split second I understand why I didn't immediately recognize him. He has grown a fierce mustache, and his face is very tan. Coupled with his civilian clothes, his disguise is complete, and he is not the man I knew in Stony Point. . . . His eyes dart alertly about the room, rest on Stacey, and then he is gone. The deputy and the guards suspect nothing, for, as in all courtrooms, some-one is continually opening the door a crack, peering in, and leaving.

Stacey sits in outward calm, but he has seen his pal, for his eyes are throwing off danger signals. He yawns, then scrubs his moist hands with his bandana. Crazily I recall that men yawn when they are excited. I, too, yawn.

The courtroom clock booms out the dragging sec-onds. I squirm in my chair and wish fervently that Joyce were not here. At any moment, the courtroom

door may fly open and a horde of machine gunners
invade the room. For that will be the only possible
way the escape can be effected; I recall the single elevator and the three flights of stairs. Someone will
die. I don't want it to be Joyce or the boys or me.
The guards are heavily armed and won't hesitate to
draw their guns and start shooting, for if they thwart
an escape, immediate reward will await them. . . .
Garsky had a crazy idea.

Then a self-starter whirs noisily. I peer out the
window. Klein, standing against the wall behind me,
drawls, "Thinking of jumping out? Go right ahead.
There's a nice concrete driveway down there to splash
on." He and Hultman chuckle at his wit.

But I do not reply, scarcely hear him, for Garsky's
red sedan is moving away from the curb, and I experience a feeling of thankfulness. He has seen the fool-
hardiness of attempting an escape in the face of such
overwhelming odds. No blood will be spilled. The
lives of Joyce and the boys and Stacey are safe.

But the red car cuts from the center of the street
into the driveway that passes beneath the windows, out
of my range of vision.

The judge enters the courtroom and mounts the
bench. The bailiff pounds his gavel. Everyone rises,
and as though our movement is a signal, an automobile
horn screams three sharp blasts from the driveway
below.

Stacey is suddenly a streak of precisioned motion.
Before the thought has fully registered in my mind,

he is clambering through the nearest window and has
flung himself into space. The officers fall all over
themselves, but Stacey wasn't too quick for Jerry. The
speedgun flashed while Stacey poised on the ledge. . . .
A ripping crash rises from the driveway.

The guards rush for the window. Klein stumbles
in his haste. He falls, and his mouth smacks sicken-
ingly against the edge of the counselors' table. Guns
appear in the hands of the other officers.

Then I see the red sedan, a great hole obliterating
the white splash on its top, as it careens into the
street. Jerry grabs another picture as the car gathers speed.

Guns start popping. The car, gaining terrific momentum, skids around a corner. The deputy warden,
four of the guards and the newspapermen make a
wild dash for the door. Joyce remains behind, with
me. The judge scampers down from the bench, and,
with the bailiff, the two attorneys and the court at-
taches, watches the scene from the window. Hultman
pushes me away from the danger area.

He mutters, "He's gone," and pockets his pistol and
helps the fallen Klein to his feet. Blood runs down
the injured guard's chin. He fingers his mouth and
brings away two broken teeth. Frozenly he gets out
his handkerchief, and sops blood from his mouth, and
eyes the street.

"Yes," he croaks stupidly, "he's gone."

"Can you beat that?" Hultman asks dazedly. "He got
clean away. Couldn't happen again in a million years."

Joyce's eyes are shining. "Yes, he got away, all right."

Hultman snaps the handcuffs on my wrist. "We won't lose you, anyway."

Joyce takes my free hand.

Hultman tugs on the cuffs.

"Stay up here and get your angle on the story," I advise Joyce. "I'll write Sunday."

With Hultman pulling me toward the door, there can be no good-by kiss. Joyce's face is white and anxious, though her eyes are hopeful. . . . I wave a feeble farewell.

Klein says, "First escape. . . . Wonder if it'll mean our jobs."

Hultman says, "Naw. We brought our man in and are taking him back, ain't we?"

We get on the elevator.

14

THE guards take me directly to the tailor shop, where they leave me. Dale brings my prison clothes. The screw is back in the laundry; Dale pulls the shades, then takes a chance on talking.

"Did he make it?"

I nod and hurriedly give him the details. He grins evilly, and his beady little eyes snap.

He snarls through his teeth, "That's the first one. Show that dirty Warden Tang a thing or two. . . . And it won't be the last, either. Stacey's just the start."

"Watch your step. If word gets around you're planning a break, Tang'll throw you in the hole and keep you there."

"Don't worry about me, kid," Dale mutters self-satisfiedly. "I've engineered these things before; I know what I'm talking about and who I'm talking to."

"Jiggers, the screw."

Dale picks up the clothes I've discarded and ducks back into the laundry.

I don my uniform, report to Captain Temple, and receive a pass to the shop. Red is all eyes. I take a chance on getting caught, clasp my hands, and nod. Carlisle sees me, but I feel so swell about Stacey's having made it that I don't give a damn if the rat does

162

turn me in to Mooney. . . . The picture of Stacey
and Garsky speeding away, with my freedom possibly
held in the palms of their hands, is something I'll carry
with me to the grave.

Then Squires, the young guard who covers our end
of the shop when he isn't on the stand, pokes me and
asks, "How'd the trial come out?"

I tell him of the escape. His eyes bug. He demands all the details, then observes, "Doesn't look like
a lucky break to me. Looks more like something
that had damn careful planning. . . . Have you told
Mooney?"

"No."

"I'll go do it."

I see them talking together on the stand; then
Mooney beckons me. Again I have to recount all the
details.

"It stinks," barks Mooney, "and from the looks of
it, you had your nose in it pretty deep."

I protest, but he waves me back to our machine.
I climb up beside the box, start the machine, and go
to work. Hunter, a banker doing a ten-year rap, has
taken Mueller's place. He and Red pull the bales out
and weigh them.

Then I see Carlisle and Mooney talking together on
the stand. Mooney glowers, stares hard toward our
machine, and writes a pass. Carlisle changes his
clothes and leaves the shop. I think, "Oh, oh—what's
this?" Red and Hunter raise their eyebrows ques-
tioningly.

In about five minutes, Billie, the deputy warden's runner, brings a pass to the shop. Mooney motions for me to put on my uniform. Red steps to the box to take my place. He mutters between clenched teeth, "If you're in a jam, kid, sit tight. Don't admit nothing."

Warden Tang is in the deputy's private office. This is the first time I've ever really seen him. A short, powerfully-built man with a face like a granite crag— hard and cruel. Now I know more than ever why the inmates hate him.

Armstrong sits by his desk and eyes me silently. The warden paces up and down the room. Hultman and Klein stand beside the deputy's desk. And seated in the corner is Carlisle.

Suddenly Warden Tang grabs my coat collar and slams me against the wall.

"Smart newspaper guy, hey?" he cries. "Where'd Stacey lam to?"

"I don't know."

"Don't lie to me, you dirty rat! I've been dealing with people like you for the last twenty-five years." He beats a tattoo against the wall with my head. "Where is he?"

"I don't know."

"Who helped him engineer this?"

"I didn't see any more than the guards and the deputy did."

Bam! My head smacks against the wall.

"You're a liar. You helped him stage it. This man saw you when you were cooking it up."

Carlisle stands and dramatically points his finger.
"He's the guy that pulled it. And he helped frame
Ludke's killing too."

I start to say, "Why, you lying rat—" but the
warden gives me another clout.

"You listen to me, you rotten son-of-a-bitch. We
know the whole story, and we're going to bury you in
that hole for the next twenty years, take away your
good time, and give you another three years for aiding
in an escape. . . . Where'd Stacey go?"

I shake my head. His grip chokes me, and I can't
talk. He flings me hard against the wall. His face
is purple with rage.

"Wise-guy newspaperman, hey?" he barks. "Think
you're still working for that dirty rag. Think you're
going to give them more dirt to write about me."

"I don't know any more about the escape than you
do."

He starts to strangle me. The deputy warden says,
"Easy, Mr. Tang."

The warden cries, "The stinking bastard! Ruin my
record, will he?" But he releases his grip.

"He engineered the whole thing, warden," says Carlisle. "I saw it all, just like I told you. When Stacey
got sent to the hole, Ross was down in back of the
breaker with Stacey not five minutes before. They
were talking and scheming something together; then
they shook hands, and Ross got a pass to Mr. Armstrong's office and ratted on Stacey. He helped Stacey
kill my pal Ludke, and then he helped him get away

and ruin your record for never having had an escape."
With the cunning of the animal for which he is named,
the rat rubs salt into the warden's wounds.

"You heard that!" yells Tang. "D' you think I'm
a fool? Stacey sent you up here to rat on him. How
else could he do it? He couldn't rat on himself."

I shake my head.

Suddenly the warden becomes as smooth and deadly
as sulphuric acid. He speaks softly. "Then how's it
happen you start stooling all of a sudden when you
never opened your mouth before?"

"It looked like a chance to get out of here. I figured
the pardon board might give me a break."

Armstrong removes a frayed cigar from his mouth.
"How'd it happen to take so long for you to figure
that out? You waited long enough before coming to
see me."

I've always been a poor liar. I decide to shut up.
They can't do any more than kill me anyway.

"I can see that board giving you a break if you
don't come clean and tell us where Stacey went and
who took him away," says the warden, his anger flaming up again. "You'll be lucky if you don't get a life
sentence for helping him kill Ludke, and I'll see that
you do every day of it in the hole."

I say nothing. I have no fears on that score, or
any other, as long as I keep my mouth shut.

"Do you have the guts to imply you didn't know
the break was all planned?" demands the warden.
"Mean to say that it wasn't figured beforehand? It

was timed right to the second. Planned out months in advance. Stacey killed Ludke just so he'd get a chance to lam from the courthouse. He cooked it up between you and some outside help—probably a former con. Stacey couldn't snitch on himself. That's where you came in. After Stacey's other pal went out and got things set on the outside, you were to snitch." The warden advances on me again. "Who helped him on the outside?"

"I don't know anything about it."

Bam! He slugs me across the mouth. My teeth cut into my lips, and I taste blood. But I must not strike back. It would mean sure death. . . . More than one inmate has been killed for beating up an officer. And what chance would I have with three others and the deadly rat Carlisle in the room?

"You don't know anything about it. Maybe this'll refresh your memory." Bam! My head spins. "Who filled the back seat of that stolen car with mattress padding so Stacey could jump into it without hurting himself?"

"I've told you everything I know."

Bam! My eye this time.

"Who took the wooden ribs from the top of the car? You don't know. Who passed Stacey a signal so he'd know when to jump and which window to jump from? You don't know that either. What kind of a car'd they change to when they ditched the stolen car down the road? You don't know anything." He slams me hard against the wall and his fist smacks my mouth again.   Things start going black.

The warden turns to the deputy.   "Throw him in the hole.   Work on him.   Knock his teeth out.   Keep him there till he talks.   If he doesn't talk, throw the key away.   Let him do every day of his time in there. Take him into court.   Get him three more years." He's roaring mad—doesn't know what he's saying. His fury is consuming him.

The deputy eyes me quizzically for a moment, chewing on his cigar.   One eye is half shut, but the disgusted look that came to his face when I snitched on Stacey is gone. . . . Armstrong, too, is furious at having a prisoner escape—the first one in the history of the prison—but though he may now despise me for aiding in ruining that record, he no longer hates me for being a rat. . . . And there's nothing they can prove against me.   I must remember that during the black days or weeks to come.

The deputy calls Captain Temple, who takes my arm roughly and shoves me toward the solid steel door that opens into the hole.   I try to explain to the captain, but he is strictly impersonal and interrupts me in the middle of my explanation.

"Take off all your clothes."

I strip to the skin.   He inspects my hands, then has me raise my arms so he can examine my armpits for hidden contraband.   Next I must lean over so he can see that there is nothing concealed between my legs. At last he is satisfied and marches me between the win-

dows and the row of solitary cells. Each is sealed by
a heavy oak door, which is equipped with a slot-hole
that can be opened from the outside for inspecting the
cell. Behind each wooden door is the conventional
steel gate.

The captain opens one of the oak doors and unlocks
a cell. He shoves me in. The cell door clangs shut.
The wooden door slams. I am in almost absolute
darkness. A faint mist of light from the outside
windows penetrates the cell from the air hole high in
the ceiling.

I feel my way about the cell. It is bare—not even
a cot to sleep on. No water tap, no light, no toilet. . . .
Oh, yes—here is a bucket in the corner. Once a day,
it will be emptied. The pail is my toilet. And there
is no cover.

But what of the chaining to the bars, about which
I've heard so much? Every inmate that's been in the
hole has told me that he's been chained to the bars
of the gate during working hours. Maybe I'm getting a break. Maybe they've forgotten to chain me
up. . . . I sit on the concrete floor and shiver in my
nakedness.

Then the oak door swings back. It is Captain Temple and Billie the runner. Billie shoves a suit of
underwear, a pair of socks and a coat and trousers
through the bars.

"Put 'em on," says the captain.

I fumble around with the underwear and manage
at last to get it on—long two-piece stuff. Then I find

that there are no buttons or strings on it.   They have been cut off as a precaution of some sort.   I pull on the trousers and don the coat.   They too are minus buttons and strings.   I become conscious of a hard lump in one of the pockets.   Billie winks clandestinely, and I feel better.   I have a friend.

"Stick your hands through the bars," says the captain.

Fat chance of their forgetting to handcuff me.

I hold my hands out, through the bars.   The captain snaps on handcuffs, closes the oak door, and I'm in the dark again.

By squirming and twisting, I get around so I can work the lump out of my pocket.   It's a tobacco can, with the makings, cigarette papers and a "buzzer" inside.   The latter is a small tin salve box that contains a steel button on a loop of string, a piece of emery and a pinch of "punk"—charred handkerchief cloth. The inmates make the punk by setting the cloth afire, letting it burn brightly for a couple of seconds, and then smothering it between the pages of a book before the cloth has turned to ash.   Then it is powdered and kept in the salve box.   To light a cigarette, you place the emery paper in the little box, on top of the punk, holding the tin in your left hand.   Then you put one end of the looped string in your mouth and hold the other in your right hand.   When you pull and release the string, the steel button spins across the emery paper and strikes a spark, which falls in the punk. The stuff glows immediately and you can get a light.

But the captain of the solitary or the night captain makes the rounds every half hour, night and day, and you have to be careful.

I roll a cigarette and buzz up. Just as I'm finishing the cigarette, I hear footsteps outside coming down the corridor, and toss the snipe into the corner. The captain opens the door. Billie has a pair of soft sneakers in his hand. He puts them on my feet. I shan't have to stand there barefoot, anyway. The door closes.

I lean against the bars, easing the handcuffs so they won't cut into my wrists, and ponder over what lies ahead. . . . From what the warden said, Stacey's escape went through without a hitch. He and Garsky evidently ditched the red sedan I saw—a hot car—at some near-by point and sped away in another car. That packing of the rear seat with padding was a smart move, as was the removal of the wooden ribs in the top. Garsky and Stacey didn't overlook a thing when they planned this.

And now I wonder if Stacey is going to work on my case. A man with the underworld connections he has shouldn't have any trouble learning who framed me and who the two young gorillas were who handled the mechanical end. . . . Even if Bill fails to get any information from Limpy down in California, Stacey can probably find out just exactly what we must know before I can expect a pardon or a parole. I'm sunk now with both boards anyway. He mentioned being able even to deliver the pair that took me for the ride that

night. If he can, my case should be a cinch, and a
new trial not even necessary.

Now I'm sure of a set-back before I can see the
parole board. I won't be interviewed until next April
instead of December. This trip to the hole takes care
of that. Unless the warden was bluffing and thinks
that I'll talk if he keeps me in here for a while. I'll
know at four o'clock this afternoon whether this is a
bluff, for at that time the count is made, and each prisoner must be accounted for as in either the hole, the
hospital, his cell or the detention ward. A daily report is sent to the board of control. I don't think the
warden would dare falsify that report, for the board
makes flying trips to the prison occasionally, and things
wouldn't look so well for the administration if conditions were found to differ from the report.

The cell is cold and clammy, and a thousand thoughts
take form, made the more fearful and dreary by the
condition of the cell. . . . Suppose Bill Mason's trip
to Los Angeles to interview Limpy turns out to be a
wild goose chase. We can't really expect to learn anything from Limpy. I'm not even sure that it was he
I saw out of the corner of my eye that morning so
long ago. And even if it was Limpy, chances are he
didn't even notice anything wrong. And even if he
had, he probably won't even know who the pair were,
for I don't think the aldermen or the car dealer would
have been fools enough to hire local hot-shots, when
plenty of good ones who'd never been seen in these

parts could be imported from the East, thus eliminating any possibility of a slip-up.

No, I'll have to depend pretty much on Stacey, and so will the paper, if it wishes to save that million dollars in lawsuits. . . . But I'm in a turmoil wondering if Stacey will really get to work on my case, now that he's out. It's a lot to ask. He shouldn't stay around these parts. He and Garsky should beat it far away, or they'll be caught. . . . And I've heard so many men promise to help others in the prison, once they were free. But when their time was up, they forgot all about the men they promised to help. No word ever came back from them. . . . Everything looks so simple from within the prison, but aiding to free a man, either legally or otherwise, is not so readily accomplished. Men make promises when they're in here, and mean them. But once they're outside, the prison drops from them like an old suit. They don't want to think about the place or do anything that reminds them of what they left behind. And they're hard at work trying to re-establish themselves. They forget their promises. . . . The black thoughts creep closer around me, and I'm sure I'll hear nothing from Stacey. More certain with the passage of each moment, as other obstacles to my release rise in my mental path. It's up to Bill and Lew and Joyce. And they've been unable to do anything so far. I guess I'm sunk.

The oak door opens. It is Armstrong. He eyes me for a moment. And then, "I suppose you know how you stand around here now." I nod.

"I'll give you this one last chance," he continues. "If you'll let me have the lowdown on Stacey's escape, tell me who helped him and where we may be able to find him, I'll let you out of here and give you your first-grade stripe."

"I don't know anything about it."

"You know what this'll mean. Nine months before you can see the parole board, and good-by to any chance of getting a break from them when you do see them."

"They'll give me plenty of time anyway," I say.

"Not if I put in a word for you. They won't have to know you were mixed up in this at all; they'll just think you helped solve it."

I shake my head. "Nothing doing. Grayce is chairman of the board, and he hates my guts anyway. He wouldn't give me a break if I saved his mother's life."

"This is the last time you'll be offered a chance. When the four o'clock count goes in, we'll have to report you as either in or out of the hole, and we'll have to give the reason if you're still in here."

After five months in Stony Point, I finally blow up. "The hell with all this stuff. I'm in here on a bum rap, and I don't care what you do. I didn't commit any crime and I don't see why I've got to obey your rules. You won't get a word out of me. And let me tell you something else. I'm not taking a thing from anybody around here any more. Rules don't mean a thing. I'll talk when I please, and slug the first guy, con or otherwise, who crosses me. I'm tired of being a sheep and trying to get along till I can get out. If I'm going to stay here a long time, I'm at least going to be comfortable. A blind man could see that it doesn't do any good to try to keep from getting in bad or blowing your good time. From now on, I'm going to be just as mean and dirty and hard to handle as the worst louse in the joint. I don't know where Stacey lammed to, but I'm glad he made it, and I wouldn't tell where he was if I knew and you promised me a pardon and ten thousand bucks to boot."

I expect to get another cuffing, figuring it's worth it to let off steam that's been trying to escape for five months, but Armstrong just stands outside my cell and listens to me rave without raising a hand or making any remonstrance. When I finally run down, I'm so mad I can't hold back the tears. The deputy shakes his head.

"You're about the last man I expected to blow up like this. I thought you had sense enough to know that such an attitude doesn't hurt anyone but yourself. You ought to remember that it doesn't make a bit of difference to us whether you're locked up in solitary all the time or working in the shops. And you should remember that you were sent here to be punished. Whether or not you're guilty is no affair of ours. That's up to the courts and the pardon board. I told you that the first day you came here. We have to assume that everyone who comes here is guilty. If we didn't, and started discriminating, the place would be a madhouse. . . . But whether or not you're guilty doesn't alter the fact that you have no right to aid in a jailbreak. If we could prove it, you could get another three years. So I'm giving you a big break when I offer to turn you out of here and give you your first-grade stripe if you'll give us the information we want." He pauses a moment until I can quit sobbing and can get hold of myself. "It'd be pretty darn nice to go up and see the parole board in time to be home for Christmas."

I stand silently, handcuffed to the bars.

"Well, speak up. Do you want to go home for Christmas, or stay here, locked in the hole?"

I mutter, "I. haven't a thing to say."

The deputy slams the door. I ease the handcuffs back from my wrists, where they had tightened and started to cut during my momentary insanity. . . . Now I am in for it. Nine more months to wait before I can see the parole board. And maybe Stacey won't even lift a finger to get me out. Maybe he couldn't if he wanted to. . . . But that lawyer—Lockhart—he'd promised. Yes, but maybe he's in trouble because of the escape; maybe the authorities figure he had a hand in it and locked him up. Nuts! Don't be a dope. You're trying to scare yourself. Smart criminal lawyers don't get in trouble like that. They've always got an out. And besides from what was seen in the courtroom, nobody could ever in a thousand years hang anything on him. . . . He'll be down to see you . . . Maybe . . . You hope. . . .

And then there's that rat Carlisle—what's eating him? The guy must be stir-nuts already. Cracking that you had it in for him and helped Stacey bump Ludke off. Screwy as a loon. You wouldn't dirty your hands killing people like that—wouldn't even smack him with your fists. . . . Maybe Red'll bump Carlisle off before you're out of the hole.

Well, here you are, in the hole, and doing twenty years for a crime you didn't commit. And even a powerful daily can't help you—can't help itself, as far as that's concerned, with a million bucks and its future existence at stake. . . . If you were a crook or were really responsible for those people getting killed, it wouldn't be so bad. You'd expect to do some time if you were caught. But you're not a crook or a killer. You're just a dumb newspaper guy who was dopey enough to think he could beat a political machine. . . . On the outside, you'd be the first one to help expose crime. You wouldn't help a crook do anything wrong in a million years. Instead, you'd run the story down and slap it all over the paper. Yet the joint has got you so bad now that you risk years of imprisonment rather than do now what any good citizen would consider his duty. You've even got so you hate all the good citizens in the world—all those taxpayers and grass mowers and yard sprinklers whose votes put crooks in office. Dumb, hard-working citizens! You'll always hate their guts because they're the blind, igno-rant, slow-witted crackpots they are.

When you first came here, you imagined that every
day would bring your release.   Then you started figuring in weeks.   Then months.   And now you're beginning to feel it's nearly hopeless.   And you hate all
the world and God and Jesus Christ for letting you
in for a mess like this.   You don't want any part of
them. . . . When you came here, you had no intention
of adopting the code of the convict.   But now you're
not only a convict by number and garb; you're also
a convict at heart.   That's what the dumb taxpayers
and yard sprinklers and grass mowers and God and
Jesus Christ and all the rest of the world have done
for you.   That's what prison has made of you.   The
hell with all of them.

In the drawer of my writing desk at home is a completed manuscript and several stories that are unfinished.   Like every newspaperman since the game was
born, I had intended to write the Great American
Novel. Tomorrow. Too busy today. But tomorrow, without fail.   I'd startle the world when I put
my thoughts on paper and submitted them to the eyes
of a publisher.   But now I fear that all this sorrow
and misery and silence have dried me up inside.   Nothing seems worth the effort.   I can't realize that it was
really I, Frank Ross, who once worked sporadically
on those stories that lie in the drawer at home.   It
seems as if I was then some disembodied soul that
could hover above the shoulders of others and watch
them at their tasks and play.   For the past life of

Frank Ross is an unreal thing, more like a dream or the happenings of somebody else than reality. I feel as if I was born on the yesterday that I entered this prison; before that I didn't exist, and all the memories I have are either half-forgotten dreams or the actions of someone else. . . . The thought suddenly strikes me that maybe I'm getting a little crazy. This staring into the dark, staring at nothing and thinking black thoughts——

The door opens. It is the captain.

"Cuffs off for lunch." He sets a piece of bread and a cup of water on the crossbars.

"How long before you put them back on again?" I ask, rubbing my chafed wrists.

"Half an hour. You wear them during working hours."

That means from eight in the morning till noon and from 12:30 till 4:30. Eight long hours of standing at the bars, unable to move about at all.

I ask the captain about using the pail.

"Do it when you have the cuffs off or you're out of luck," he says.

"But," I protest, "what if I have to go anyway?"

"Then do it in your pants." He closes the door. Son-of-a-bitch. He sounds like a second lieutenant.

Five months ago I hardly ever swore. Now swearing is a part of my thoughts.

I start pacing the floor of my cell, munching pieces of the bread and sipping from the cup of water. I wonder what Joyce is doing now—what plan of action

Bill has—how the picture came out that Jerry grabbed of Stacey jumping out the window. . . . It'll be a long time before I can go through the old files at the office and see those pictures and read the story. Unless Stacey——

But I mustn't dwell on my predicament so much. I'll go nuts for sure.

Home—on the table in my room is a typewriter, and along one wall is a bookcase. I can remember most of the books on those shelves. My old schoolbooks on journalism and writing, my dictionaries, the thesaurus, a bunch of novels. No Shakespeare, no classics. For some reason I never cared for them. Too much descriptive matter to suit me. . . . From my window I can see the poplars, the elms, the bridal-wreath and the hedge around my mother's yard. My dog barks. A streetcar rattles past.

I wonder what my mother will do when she receives no letters from me for the next thirty days—what Joyce will do. What I will do, not hearing from them. I shan't even know whether Bill has any success with Limpy in Los Angeles. Not for a month. It's going to be a living hell during that time, not knowing, just guessing and hoping, but fearing in my heart that everything is getting blacker with the passage of each day.

My mother will be the one to suffer the most, though. Mothers always are. She's home alone with Charles, and has nothing but her thoughts for comfort—thoughts and an empty home.

Home, your cords are bound tight around my heart. Home, you seem like some vanished castle. Walls that creak and floors that whisper. Ground that sprouts the seeds I planted. Nooks and corners steeped in memories. Winds that sigh beneath the eaves. Home——

I fear that I shall never see you again. You have become a dim, fogged illusion that sweeps in and out of my mind, sometimes faint, sometimes strong, but always growing less real, like a book once read and long forgotten—a memory like a dream, a dream like a memory. No more will your floors echo my footsteps, your stairs creak a protest at my weight. . . . Twenty years. Home, when I left you, I was young, and life was good. There was a God in Heaven, and a new adventure awaited me each day. Now I feel like an old man who has seen too much of life and is tired of living. . . . God, if you're really up there, tell me whether Stacey or Bill or somebody'll get me out of here. I think I'm going nuts.

Outside the prison walls are three poplar trees whose crowns rise like a spray of emerald against the sky. And poplars were always somehow included in my dreams. I liked to believe that some day I'd have sons like those trees—tall and straight and fine. But now I don't know. The future looks black. The months in prison have done something to me.

The oak door swings back and lets in a flood of light.

"All right, Ross," says the captain. "Stick your mitts out and I'll give you a little present."

The handcuffs snap on for another four hours.

15

I am beginning my eleventh day in the hole. I am becoming very weak. When the handcuffs are removed at noon and at night, I can't pace my cell for more than a few moments. My mind wanders in fantastic circles, as though I am on the border of insanity. . . . Last night I imagined my mother was here. I told her of my hopes that have been killed and my plans that will never see completion. And she held me in her arms and cried over me. And I was almost happy, for I believed that everything I am going through was only á bad dream, and that I was a little boy again. . . . Then the oak door opened, the night captain peered in, and life resumed its chaotic pattern.

Once, during the past ten days, Billie managed to smuggle a sandwich in to me. But that was nearly a week ago. My tobacco is gone. I can't eat the bread. It sticks in my throat when I try to swallow it and chokes me. Each day the prison physician makes the rounds of the solitary cells and inquires as to the health of the men. At first I complained to him, feeling that we were both college men with a profession. I was sick and weak. My nerves were shot to pieces. But I soon learned that no protest was worth the effort. His visits are merely a gesture, gone through emptily

182

in compliance with the rules of the board of control. . . . Each time I drink water I shiver and retch. My circulation is poor. My bowels haven't móved for five days. Occasionally, when I am not chained to the bars, I rise from the floor and stumble back and forth for a few moments. The exertion weakens me doubly, but warms me up for a little while.

But I have hopes of being released today. As I recall from snatches of conversation I remember having had with other inmates, there's some sort of law about not keeping a man in solitary on bread and water for over ten days. Maybe I'll be taken out soon.

While the thought is still registering, the warden opens the oak door. I peer at him. The light from the window across the corridor is blinding. Behind him is the deputy. It is the warden's first visit to me since he ordered me thrown into the hole—the deputy's third.

"Ready to talk yet?" growls the warden.

"There's nothing to say," I mutter. "I've told everything I know."

He slips a key into the lock of the cell door.

"Get out of there. You're going to work, by God. Laying around here on your dead fanny! Get going."

"To work? No fooling?"

"Get the hell out of there!"

I cover my eyes and step from the cell. The warden shoves me ahead of him. I fall, then reel slightly as

I regain my feet. My head is spinning. All I can say or think is, "Thank God! Thank God!"

I feel as though I am treading on air as I make my way to the bathroom. No officer is there, but one inmate is mopping the floor. He slides over to me as I get under the shower. It is Dale.

"Nice work, Ross. Stacey got clean away."

I try to smile.

He says, "I'll getcha your clothes."

While he is in the tailor shop, I scrub myself. The water feels good—clean and refreshing—and puts new life and strength into me. I gulp a few swallows from the needle spray. The water stings my eyes. Then I dry myself and sit on the long bench in front of the showers and wait for Dale.

He places a mound of clothes beside me.

"Was Billie able to take care of you while you was in the hole?" he asks.

"Twice. He fixed me with tobacco and a buzzer the first day and got me a lump a few days later. I guess he couldn't make it with anything after that."

"No. You're hot as hell around here. Tang figures it would take a newspaper guy to dope out all the details of an escape like that, and he blames you for the whole thing. He's damn near nuts from the way the papers've been riding him over Stacey's caper."

"The hell with him," I say.

"The hell with him is right," whispers Dale. "Him and all the rest of his dirty rat screws. I can't stand this joint no longer. I'd rather be in the nut house.

I'm gonna figure out something, just like I told you before."

"What you figuring on?" I ask.

"This joint ain't as escape-proof as it's cracked up to be. That's all the old bull, just to keep us from trying. I'll figure out an angle, and there'll be a lot of cons hitting the bricks one of these days."

"You'll never make it without outside help."

"Don't worry; I'll have it. . . . I'm just in here for knocking off that whore, but that don't mean I ain't got dough on the outside. I pulled plenty after I lammed from Chelan. That dough'll get me a connection for some guns."

"Guns! How'll you ever connect for them in here?"

"There's ways if you got dough. I'll finance this thing, and we'll all be out as soon as I get everything arranged."

"You're stir-nuts, Dale. You'll never make it."

"Stacey did. So can we."

"That couldn't happen again in a million years."

"I don't mean the way he pulled it. There's a party going out in April. He'll get the guns if I fix him with some dough."

April! I heave a sigh of relief. I'll probably be long gone from here by then. And Dale will have awakened from his pipe dream.

Dale whispers dangerously, "Just put a gat in my hand! I'll be running the show then, and I'll bump off a lot of people that have it coming to them. And

I'll be financing the thing; I've got it all figured out; these cons'll do as I say or else." ·

"Better pipe down about it," I warn, humoring him. "It might get back to Tang or Armstrong."

"Just the same, I'm fed up with the joint. It's too tough, and lamming's my only chance." He swings the talk back to me. "But you're the guy that wants to look out for Tang. He ain't got nothing on you, but he hates newspapermen anyway ever since that lumber stink, and he'll try to make it plenty tough for you."

"Phooey—he's got nothing on me, and he'll play hell trying to frame me. One frame is enough."

"I mean he'll have Mooney and his rat riding you all the time, and you'll spend most of your time in the hole and third grade."

Mad Dog Mooney! Queer I hadn't thought of him before. Working in his shop will be almost as bad as being in the hole.

"I'll beat that rap," I decide. "I won't go to work till I'm out of third grade. Then I'll write the board of control. They won't stand for having us ridden, but we get in bad here for writing. . . . I'll write them anyway, and I'll do the third-grade time in D.W."

"Good idea. . . . You hungry now?"

"Oh, Jesus!"

"Wait a second. I'll go score a lump. . . . But keep your trap shut about the break. I engineered one in Chelan, and I can do it again here, if it doesn't get to the rats while I'm lining up men."

I nod and start pulling on the clothes. In a moment
he returns from the tailor shop with a can of sardines
and a piece of ginger cake.

"Here, throw these into you."

I open the can and gulp down the cake and the fish.
Dale goes to the sink and gets me a tin cup full of
water. I feel a lot better. Stronger and cleaner.

"Where'd you score the food?" I ask.

"Pat's a waiter in the dining room. He scores lots
of grub for us. There's always something hid around
the tailor shop."

He means Pat O'Brien, the lifer who got me the
lemon juice. He's doing the book for a bank stickup.

"There's tobacco and a buzzer in your clothes," says
Dale. "Lemme know if you need anything while
you're in third grade. It's no trouble at all for Billie
to get stuff in to the guys in D. W."

I finish dressing, then enter the tailor shop. The
guard puts me in the barber chair, and the inmate
barber clips off all my hair and shaves my beard. I
feel naked and look like a skinned rat.

I put on the coat. It has three diagonal black stripes
on the left sleeve. I am in third grade. And I swore,
when I came here, I'd never do anything to lose my
grade. Now I don't care. The only thing that bothers me is the inconvenience of losing my privileges
for thirty days. No mail. No talking. Have to
sneak my smokes. And go back to the hole if I'm
caught. . . . But after being in the hole, third grade
is unconditional freedom by comparison. And only

twenty days of this before I get my second–grade rating; then I'll get most of my privileges back. The ten days in the hole count against my third-grade time.

The officer in the tailor shop looks me over and says, "You're a sergeant now. Mind your own business and I'll make you a second lieutenant. And then if you can mind it for another month, I'll give you a first lieutenant's stripe." He laughs. It is very funny to him. . . . But there's Mad Dog Mooney waiting to receive me out in the shop. He'll keep me in third grade for months—he and his rat Carlisle.

I march across the hall into the deputy warden's office. The warden is there. He scowls at me and barks, "What the hell you want? Why haven't you gone to the shop?"

"Do I have to work for Mooney?"

"You're damn right you do. We've got other ways than the hole to make men talk."

"Then lock me up in D.W.," I say. "I'm not working till I'm out of third grade. And after that I'm writing the board of control."

His face purples. "You're what!"

"I'm not being a damn fool any longer. I've got people on the outside, and you're not getting away with riding me when I haven't done anything you can prove. I'll write the board, and my mother and my editor'll see them. My mother may not know much about prison regulations, but the editor's not so dumb."

"Why, you——" He smacks me one with his balled fist and I fly back against the wall. The warden turns to the deputy. "Throw him back in the hole! Keep him there for the rest of his third-grade time. . . . And from now on if anybody refuses to work after coming out of the hole, place a new report against him and toss him back in."

At noon, the oak door swings back, and the deputy stands there with Billie. The runner slides a full meal to me, through the bars, while the deputy removes the cuffs from my wrists.

"You're getting this meal in compliance with the rules of the board of control," says the deputy. "You've already had a bath and been out of your cell, and you'll get the same thing after another ten days of this. Remember that when you write the board."

"Don't worry," I say. "When I write, the warden won't let the letter go out."

"When you get your grade, you'll be allowed to write the board, the same as any other inmate. And your letter'll go out. . . . Are you getting so screwy you have an idea we're afraid of you? You've brought all this on yourself. We're not such damn fools we don't know who was behind that break. We may not be able to prove it till we catch Stacey, but we'll catch him eventually. You know that. And then your troubles will be just starting."

"I'll sit here and worry about it."

"You'd better sit here and get yourself back together. You weren't a bad prisoner before you mixed up with Stacey, but the way you're going now, you'll spend the rest of your life in joints like this "

"Deputy," I cry, "can't you understand the way I feel? I'm doing twenty years for a crime I didn't commit. The pardon board won't help me. The administration hates my paper, so the sheet can't do a thing with the Governor. I'm here through no fault of my own, and all I've got since I came here has been tough breaks and abuse. . . . First it was Pete Kassock and those rats, Ludke and Carlisle. Now it's Mooney and Carlisle. They'll have me in third grade for twenty years. And I shouldn't even be in prison. Can you blame me for hating the joint and everyone in it?"

"We've gone through all that before. You're sent down here for us to watch and discipline. Regardless of what my personal feelings may be, every inmate is guilty and gets the same treatment as the rest."

"Like hell," I object. "Look at that Carlisle rat. Nothing but a dirty snitch, and the screws give him the best jobs in the place."

Armstrong turns to Billie. "All right. You can go." After the runner has left, the deputy says, "Carlisle tells me he's afraid you're going to try to frame him or kill him."

"That guy's the craziest loon I've ever heard of. If he's got any idea I'm going to frame him or hurt him, you can put his mind at rest. I've got troubles enough of my own, even though he caused most of them."

The deputy nods. "That's what I thought."

"Does the warden really think I had anything to do with that Ludke killing?"

"No.   He was upset that day when a twenty-five-year record went up in smoke. . . . To tell you the truth, Ross, I don't personally believe you're guilty of the rap you're serving this time for.   I followed the case in the papers, and it looked to me as if a hell of a lot was left out.   But that's just my personal opinion. If you're not guilty, it'll come out in the end.   Bound to. . . . Now, I can't turn you out of here, nor can I discriminate in your favor.   But I'll see that the favoritism is stopped if I find that some is actually being shown.   You know I can't turn you loose, but I can do this much until you get a break: If you'll keep your nose clean, once you're out of the hole, I'll see that no bum raps stick against you.   You'll get no marks and you won't be put back in the hole unless you've got it coming to you.   You deserved what you got this morning.   You won't be out of here for twenty more days.   In the meantime, you'll get a bath and a full meal at the end of ten days.   When you do come out, take some good advice and start all over again.   Forget all about pitying yourself, and concentrate on trying to improve your record so you'll get a parole.   Keep out of trouble and keep away from the troublemakers.   We've got enough of them around here as it is."

Armstrong's talk snaps me out of the frame of mind that has possessed me for so long.

"Okay, deputy.   I guess I've been a little crazy with worry."

"Get your mind off yourself.   Try to forget your troubles.   Watch your step, and you'll be out of prison before you know it."

The door closes, and I start doing the rest of my third-grade time in solitary.

I decide not to write the letter to the board of control.

16

THE thirty days of blackness and solitary isolation end at last. The door swings open. The deputy unlocks the gate. I walk out into the corridor, trying to shield my eyes from the bright sunlight that pours in the windows. Outside, I see the prison yard; the grass looks green and inviting. And tomorrow afternoon I shall be out there, for in a few moments I'll be a second-grade prisoner, with all privileges.

Armstrong says, "What the hell! How come you're walking so well after twenty days of it, when you could barely navigate after ten?"

I grin at him. "I can take it."

He scowls. "Somebody's been feeding you. Who was it?"

"Santa Claus."

"One more crack out of you and I'll have you back in the hole."

I lay off the kidding.

"Come on," persists the deputy. "Who fed you?"

Can I tell him that Billie did it? Can I tell him that Red and Dale and O'Brien and Billie stole every choice item they could lay their hands on and sneaked it in to me during the last twenty days? Another lie coming up.

"I ate all my bread, and just took it easy this time."

"I'd like to get my hands on the man who fed you," snorts Armstrong. "I'll bet I'd have his skin to hang to that wall."

I bathe, get my second-grade uniform, fiddle through an afternoon of work in the shop, and at last am in my cell, waiting for the night count to be completed. On the cot is the mound of mail that has accumulated during the last thirty days. There are letters from Joyce, my mother, Joe, Lew, Bill and Jerry. The count is completed. I dive into the mail, saving Joyce's letters until last—until the bowl of my pipe is a hot ember. Then I start slowly to trace it between the lines of each letter. And at last two lines of tiny invisible writing take form as the paper browns:

Stacey 'phoned. Has gone West. Garsky unsuspected and handling investigation this end.

I sum up the main body of her other letters. She will be down to see me soon with Lockhart the attorney, who 'phoned her that I was in solitary and could not have visitors for thirty days. Bill Mason flew to Los Angeles the day following Stacey's break, but when Bill got there and Ray Pick had taken him to Limpy's hangout, the cripple had disappeared without a trace. . . . I feel my spirits sag . . . Limpy's disappearance looks suspicious; perhaps Lockhart or one of his associates will have ways and means of locating him. The paper is getting desperate over the lawsuits. Escape of prisoner from courtroom made great copy. *Record* scooped entire country with pictures, which

made A. P. Wirephoto, coast-to-coast. . . . I get a
glow from that. It was my story, by golly—my
story—coast-to-coast. . . . Boys are all working hard
on case, though it's pretty much rechecking clews that
petered out long ago.

I undress, climb in between the sticky blankets, which
feel like silk sheets after my long siege in the hole, and
stare at the ceiling. . . . Stacey is out. He's working for me. Joyce and the attorney are coming for a
visit. Maybe I'll be going home soon. Maybe. Home.
Gosh!

I can hear the prison band blasting away from where
I stand at my cell door. Then the gong clangs its four-
toned message for the fourth gallery. We slide back
the gates, march down the steps, and line up in the
prison yard for an afternoon in the sun and fresh air.
Red can't keep his long neck in and keeps peering down
the line before the deputy signals for us to break ranks.
Then at last we're free for two hours, and the hairy
man is pounding me on the back.

"You old son-of-a-bitch, you!" he howls. "Did you
get them lumps we sent in?"

"Boy, I'll say. And were they ever life savers! A
guy could do six months in there if he took it easy and
didn't have to get by on bread and water."

"By God, it's swell to have you back. I come damn
near stickin' a shiv in that rat's guts for what he
pulled."

"Nix, Red. You've got troubles enough of your own."

Dale and O'Brien stop and shake hands.

"Nice work, Ross," says O'Brien. "It was as pretty a getaway as was ever framed. Too bad you couldn't go with him."

"We got to take care of that rat," says Fargo Red.

"Yeah," mutters Dale. "I been thinking about that. Suppose we better frame up through Billie and have a can of soda planted in Carlisle's cell?"

"Never mind, fellows," I say. "What's done is done. He thinks I've got it in for him and even told the deputy I was going to try to frame him. Skip it."

The deputy warden's hand drops on my shoulder. I figure it's more trouble, but he hands me a pass.

"Your attorney's out there to see you."

I beat it for the front gate. The pass reads "Attorney and friend on business." That will be Joyce.

They come through the gates. Joyce is in my arms, and, once again, after all the days and weeks of darkness and misery, her sweetness is something close and real. Her usually bright gray eyes are misty, but there's a happy little smile tugging at the corners of her lips.

"You made it all right," I whisper. "I was afraid they might not let you in—especially on a Saturday afternoon."

"Mr. Lockhart called the capitol this morning and got permission." Now the mist is leaving her eyes. I hold her back and look long at her—a trim little figure whose blue hat and dress belie her mood. Around her shoulders is a crisp white collar.

Then I'm shaking hands with Mr. Lockhart.

"I don't know whether or not I'm meeting you again in happier circumstances than before."

We seat ourselves, and I hold Joyce's hand while we talk.

Lockhart says, "We'll have to start right from the beginning and see if I can't pick up something that was omitted from the records. I've gone over the transcript, but understand that a lot of your side's testimony was stricken out."

I tell him all I can remember of the case. He listens carefully as I talk, prompting me with questions, taking notes and names, but depending mostly upon his memory. His black little eyes bore right into me.

"Think hard," he coaches. "Didn't you have a single glimpse of the two men who kidnaped you— didn't you catch even a momentary flash of a profile or hear a voice?"

I shake my head wearily. It's the old question I've asked myself a thousand times. "I didn't see them or hear them. All I know is that two men stuck guns in me and pushed me toward my car. I wouldn't know them if I saw them."

Lockhart nervously drums his immaculate thin fingers on his equally immaculate trousers. "Then we'll just have to surmise that they either knew you by sight and were afraid of being recognized, or that they had a lookout to finger you and were just naturally cautious. I can't believe that the former is the case, for the men who wanted you framed wouldn't be likely to use local men—too much chance of their being recognized by a newspaperman, then traced to the higher-ups. So we'll work on the second theory—that you were fingered by someone who knew you. . . . All right, a group of aldermen or an automobile dealer wouldn't be likely to have connections with hired hot shots in the East. So they'd have to make a local contact, who would do the actual work of making the connections. That ties in with our theory that you were put on the spot by someone who knew you—someone who was working with out-of-town men. . . . Did you notice anyone other than Limpy Julien on the street that morning?"

I've racked my brain over the same question, but the answer is always no.

"Then," continues Lockhart, smiling a tight, shrewd little smile, "there's nothing to do but assume that Limpy Julien was the finger man. I've looked him up pretty thoroughly, and he fits into the picture nicely. From certain sources, I learned that it's safe to call on him if you're hot, following, say, a kidnaping or a robbery. I know of three eastern mobsters who were on the dodge after a snatch, and who were holed up by Limpy. He's a smooth bird, is known not to talk, has quite a long police record, was mighty broke at the time you were framed, and suddenly broke out with a lot of money and left immediately for the West Coast.

That raises a lot of questions that are going to have to be answered as soon as we find him."

"That's not going to be so easy," I state. "Bill Mason flew to L. A. looking for him, without any luck."

"Yes, I know. But," and again he smiles that tight little smile, "we have other means of locating him. It won't be hard."

"I'm sure Mr. Lockhart can find him, Frank," ventures Joyce. She smiles. I understand without having to be hit on the head.

"Now, then," resumes Lockhart, "did he make any suspicious moves or give any signals when you left the office that morning?"

"No. That's just another one of those questions I've asked myself a thousand times."

"You'd waited around until 2:30 in the morning to see how your graft story looked—that right?"

"Yes."

"How long had the presses been running?"

"Not long. I grabbed a copy, read it, then started for home."

"Don't you think it strange that Limpy, an ex-newspaper peddler and a racketeer, would be hanging around watching the presses at that time of morning?"

"I've been figuring he just happened by and stopped for a look. . . . Nearly everybody stops to watch the papers come out."

"Not at 2:30 of a cold winter morning. He came there for a purpose. . . . At what time did you usually leave the plant?"

"About one o'clock."

"Then those men needed someone to wait with them and point you out. They couldn't have just happened by and caught you. They waited an hour and a half, knowing you'd be out. And the man who waited with them was Limpy Julien. I'll stake my life on it . . .. Oh, yes—what made you notice him standing there?"

"I don't know—I guess it was probably the contrast of his face shining out of the dark when he lit a cigarette."

"Lit a cigarette?" Lockhart turns excitedly to Joyce, his lean dark face tense and slightly angered. "No one told me of that."

"I didn't know it until just now," protests Joyce.

I falter lamely, "I'm afraid I didn't either. Your question brought the scene to life in my mind."

"Can't you see now?" asks Lockhart, tapping the tips of his fingers against his knees. "That was the signal. Julien had to make some sign that wouldn't attract attention but would tell the men when you came out. Now we're definitely on the right track." He winks slyly. "I'll have my West Coast representative track him down at once. And when we locate him, we won't take no for an answer."

"But what if you can't find him?" I ask.

"Don't worry, Ross. There's more than one way to skin a cat, as the saying goes. If we don't find him, we'll get the dope some place else. Remember this: there's at least one other man, besides Limpy Julien and the two men who framed you, who knows all about

this. And we'll find him if we have to comb the underworld of every city in the United States. It may take
time, but we'll have you out of here and exonerated."

Joyce smiles and squeezes my hand. "The paper's
lawyers are working with Mr. Lockhart now, Frank.
I know we haven't accomplished much so far, but we
evidently didn't know how to handle a situation like
this. Mr. Lockhart does. He's had to prove the
innocence of men before—a man you know, several
times. And now we'll get some place. So please
don't lose heart."

Her smile fades and anxiety stains her face.

"I'll hang on all right, Joyce. Don't worry."

"Were you put in solitary because of that Stacey
affair?" Joyce continues. The guard, who has been
sitting in a semi-trance, snaps out of it. He has evidently been given instructions to listen for hints concerning Stacey's escape.

I shake my head. "No. I didn't know anything
about that, other than what you heard in the courtroom. I got messed up and went to the hole for something else."

Joyce nods understandingly. I frown slightly.
Joyce asks, "You look so thin and white and pale.
How long were you locked up?"

The guard says, "This is a business visit. If you're
through, I'll have to send Ross back."

I shrug. Lockhart shakes my hand. I kiss Joyce
good-by. The picture of her clings to me as I head

back to the prison yard. . . . Limpy Julien. So he's
the rat at the bottom of this mess.

Red is waiting for me at the yard entrance of the
north cell hall.

"How'd it go, kid?" he demands. "Hear anything
good?"

I tell him all I dare—everything except that Stacey
has gone West and will try to find Limpy there.

Red says, "By God, that looks pretty swell fer you
then." But I can see that his words are forced, his
manner preoccupied, as though he has something
weighty on his mind.

I say, "All right, spill it, Red. What's biting you?"

He grins, squirts a brown stream into the grass,
wipes the spray from his chin, and says, "You're the
damnedest guy fer guessing things I ever seen. How'd
yuh know I had something t' tell you?"

"I'm psychic, I guess."

"You're what!"

"Never mind, Red. Skip it. I was just kidding
you."

He struts importantly. "It's about the rat, Carlisle.
I'm skeered that when he gits in his cell tonight, he's
gonna have an awful surprise waiting fer him."

"You guys planted something on him!"

"Naw! How'd yuh guess it?"

"You dirty so-and-so's!"

Red scratches his neck and lazily closes one eye.
"Yeah, I kin just imagine your pore heart's breaking."

"What'd you do?"

"Me! I didn't do nothing. Whatahell you think I am? But I know a guy that put a pretty little can of baking soda in the rat's cell. And this same party's gonna see that the deputy finds a note on his desk telling about it as soon as yard time's over and we've et supper. . . . Guy's a runner. He kin get around."

I shake my head, but don't feel so bad about it that I want to cry. "It's a dirty trick, Red, but that rat certainly asked for it."

"Boy, he's certainly gonna git it."

The whistle on top of the power house hoots its warning. All talking ceases, and we line up by shops and file into the dining hall. Carlisle somehow manages to sit beside me during the meal. As we rise and file from the table, he snarls, "Guess we tamed you some, didn't we, Mr. Newspaperman?"

Red sticks his foot out as we swing into the hallway, and Carlisle falls flat on his face. I expect Red to go to the hole, but Mac is the only screw who saw it, and curses Carlisle for clumsiness when the rat snitches on Red. All along the line, the inmates give Carlisle the silent chuckle.

That night Mac stops in front of my cell. "You see that crazy Fargo Red trip Carlisle in the hall?" he asks.

I laugh. "The rat had it coming to him. He'd just given me the horselaugh and taken credit for getting me thirty days in the hole."

"Well," drawls Mac, whirling his finger in his ear and eying me sidewise, "he won't be giving anybody else the horselaugh for a while."

"How's that?"

"The deputy just shook down his cell and found a can of soda. Yessir, your friend Mr. Carlisle's going to be in the hole for the next five or ten days. . . . But of course you wouldn't know anything about that." He smiles, his Irish face a mass of wrinkles.

"I ain't a-sayin', stranger," I crack. And add, "Have you told Red?"

"No, but I'm damn soon gonna. The whole cell hall'll know it as quick as I make my rounds with the next light."

"Listen, Mac, do me a favor, and I'll give you a good write-up in the paper when I get out."

"Baloney! You'd slander your own mother if it'd make a good story."

"Okay, pal, but go on back down to Red's cell and tell him now. It'll be just like getting a pardon for Red to hear about Carlisle."

"He'll probably jump right through the bars to kiss me," growls Mac, but nevertheless trots off toward Red's cell.

I hear them whispering for a while; then Mac's footsteps pad down the stairs.

After a few moments, Red's voice booms out: "Listen, guys! That rat Carlisle's gone t' the hole!"

It suddenly sounds as though a thousand giant firecrackers have exploded.

"HOORAY, THE DIRTY BASTARD!"

The walls rock.

17

THOUGH the rules of the prison are as strictly enforced as they were prior to Carlisle's being sent to the hole, a measure of peace has come into our lives. For the deputy kept his word—the word he gave me when I was in solitary and rebelled against the favoritism shown the prison rats.

Carlisle has been out of the hole a month—has had his second-grade rating for nearly a week—but he is no longer in our shop. As soon as he was released from his ten days in solitary, Deputy Armstrong transferred him to the blacksmith shop—"the toughest go in the joint." Now Carlisle must stand all day before the blast of a white-hot fire and feed equally hot pieces of heavy iron to the skilled blacksmiths. Red is in his glory—the proud hero of Stony Point.

We are in the yard. It is late September, and the leaves of the poplar trees beyond the north wall are showing the first tinges of autumn.

Red says, "See what the boys gimme fer sending the rat to the hole?"

He pulls a salve box from his pocket, carefully raises the top, and shows me a live cockroach.

I start laughing. "Red, you're getting screwier every day, but I don't know what I'd do without you."

"Whaddyuh mean, screwy! A guy's gotta have himself a pet or he'd go nuts in this joint, an' no kidding."

The hairy man stirs up the roach, which runs around the box in circles.

"We ought to get a couple more, Red," I say. "Then we could stage a race."

"How'd we work it?" The animal trainer is only listlessly interested.

"Well, we'd paint one red, one white, and one blue. Then we'd draw a circle in the dirt, put the roaches in it, and the first one outside the circle is the winner."

Now Red is all ears. "By God, maybe we could do a little betting on it too."

"Sure. And a good way to get a cinch winner is to feed two of the roaches plenty of sugar, and starve the other. The ones that were fed are lazy, but the hungry one'll scamper across the line in a hurry."

Red scratches his nose. "Well, I'll be a low-born louse! Where'd you ever hear of that?"

While Red is busy figuring out angles for staging a race, I peek into the box, which he holds open in his hands.

"Red," I cry woefully, "your menagerie's gone."

The hairy man sees the empty box and starts searching the ground. I watch him, trying not to explode. At last he rises sadly.

"Poor Herman," he mourns. "I jist know he's gonna git stepped on by one of these big-footed cons. . . . And he was as pretty a roach as ever scampered up a drain pipe."

"Cheer up, Red. Things are bound to get worse."

"Well, I still got my mice and my sparrows, anyway."

"Mice? Can you keep them in your cell?"

"Naw. I clout an extra piece of cheese every time we get it. At night I tie a piece on the end of a string and toss it out on the floor. Pretty soon the mice come in from the gallery. When they start nibbling on the cheese, I jerk the string and they run like hell. But they always come back. They know I wouldn't hurt 'em."

"What about the sparrows?"

"By God, they're damn near driving me nuts. You know how they come in through the bars all the time, and fly around in the corridor? Well, I used to throw a few crumbs out on the gallery, and they'd eat 'em. But now they're in there, sitting on my cross bars at five o'clock in the morning, chirping and raising a fuss till I get up and throw 'em something to eat. . . . Man can't even get his sleep in jail no more."

While I am chuckling at Red's tale of woe, Carlisle passes us and makes some remark. A couple of officers are standing near by, so Red and I must be careful what we say.

"What you belly-aching about?" growls Red.

"I'm wise to you, Ross," snarls the rat. "You think you got away with something when you helped croak my partner and framed me into the hole. But I'll get you for it before you kill me too. You watch."

"Scat, you ring-tailed bastard!" barks Red from the corner of his mouth. "Beat it before I swat you like a fly."

Carlisle retreats to the water fountain, where he joins the Wolf.

"Now there's a pair that would make swell stretcher cases," observes Red. "That Herman of mine had more man in him than those two put together."

Carlisle holds his nose. Red starts after him. I grab the hairy man.

"Nix, Red. That was for me. That screwball's got an idea I've had it in for him ever since he came here and that I'm out to get him."

"I'll git him, and the next time it won't be just to the hole he'll go. They'll lay him out on that slab at the hospital."

"Well, he lost his good job in the shop, and we're rid of him, anyway, Red."

"Now if I could just frame his rat friend, the Wolf, I'd be happy. Hard to get to that guy though. He's always around his cell or in the cell hall so Billie can't sneak into his place. . . . Can't figure out what Armstrong's thinking of, keeping that louse as the cell-hall runner."

We roam aimlessly about the yard. I ponder the while on Carlisle and his hatred of me. He's evidently going to be dangerous now, believing that it was I who helped kill Ludke and who framed him into the hole. But I don't worry much about it. Carlisle is too far removed from me to cause any damage now, other than when we are in the yard or the cell hall during recreation periods. And I can watch myself at those times. . . . Maybe this will be all over soon. Joyce writes that Limpy left a trail when he ducked from his hangout in Los Angeles. She hasn't mentioned any names, but, from what I gather, Stacey feels that he's fairly safe from capture out on the coast where he's unknown. Perhaps he'll soon have tracked Limpy down, and turned him over to Lockhart. Then I suppose Stacey will disappear entirely. But I hope Lockhart will succeed in making Limpy talk first.

As though Red is reading my thoughts, he says, "Wonder what Stacey's doing now."

"Whatever it is, it isn't time."

"Funny I never figgered that guy out fer what he was," muses Red. "I thought he was sure enough a right guy, but he done you plenty dirty when he lammed outta here and left you t' take the rap. . . . That parole board's gonna be tough as hell on you, I'm afraid."

"You've got Stacey all wrong, Red. He's okay."

"Nuts! These big shots are all alike." He stuffs his mouth with tobacco and snuff. "Look at that rat Carlisle and his side-kick Ludke. They was supposed to be a couple of hot-shot killers from the East, and they turn out to be a pair of low-born finks. Carlisle oughta be laying in the grave beside his rat partner."

"Good grief, Red, you can't class Stacey with people like that. Stacey's ace high. Always has been. I've heard of him on the outside, before I ever came to

Stony Point. . . . You want to remember he's hot as
a pistol since he escaped, and can't take too many
chances to help me."

"Phooey! He's probably forgot all about yuh.
Probably living high, wide and handsome with some
dame on that fifty or a hundred grand he was supposed
to have stashed. . . . He ain't never sent you no word
or nothing since you helped him get away."

I answer evasively, preferring to keep such things
to myself. "He'll be doing something soon."

"You hope. Maybe I'm wrong, but he's been gone
a hell of a long time, and he could at least of dropped
you a phoney post card or hired a mouthpiece that
didn't just come down here and give you a lot of big
talk and then forget all about you. . . . You ain't
never heard from that shyster again, have you?"

"No," I admit, "I haven't. But he can't do anything until Stacey locates those rats that framed me.
That may take a lot of time."

"It's already taken a hell of a lot of time. I ain't
throwing no cold towels on you, Ross, but things don't
look so hot. I think we oughta lam outta this joint.
We'll both rot around here the way things are."

"Don't be a jug-head, Red. You're up to the parole
board in March, and I'm up in April. Besides,
Stacey'll probably have me out of here before then."

"Parole board!" howls Red. "You so crazy you
really think that board'll do anything fer you? And
you going up there fer the first time? They won't
even give the long-timers a break—the guys that've

served eight or ten years. They won't give me nothing but a good long set-back, and they'll probably hand
you about two or three years—maybe more, if you're
in as bad with the gang as you say."

"You're certainly a lot of help, Red." I feel a cold
chill circulating through me at his words. I realize
that he knows nothing whatsoever of what the parole
board will do, but nevertheless his foreboding, coupled
with his years of experience in Stony Point, scare me
more than I wish to show.

"I ain't trying to get you down, Frank. It's jist
that I been around here so long I know what they'll
do. . . . They hate my guts, and I ain't kidding myself about it. They'll probably give me one of them
slips saying 'continued to expiration of sentence.' And
I've never even seen the bastards before. So why
should I kid you?" He slips into a softer vein. "You
know, Frank, you're my pal. It's hell to build yourself up to going out and then get a slap from that
board. Just like being sentenced all over. I don't
want that to happen to you. Just figure you ain't
gonna get nothing; then if they surprise you, so much
the better."

"Well," I falter, "I guess I'll just have to figure on
Stacey."

"Don't do it. I've seen them so-called big shots before. When I was in the hospital, they brung in a
guy named Humphreys—a tough mug an' a bad hom-
bre on the outside, if you'd listen t' him talk. Bank
robber doin' the book. Busted outta twenty or thirty

jails before they finally got him down here—accordin'
t' his story . . . An' then something went haywire
with his insides, an' they figgered he was gonna die.
So they put him in a quiet cell at the hospital, an' went
away, an' forgot all about him, like they do everybody
else up there. Jesus, you shoulda heard him holler!
They hadda get the croaker over there about ten times
at three or four in the morning. . . . Now I know
for sure this Humphreys bumped at least a couple of
guys on the outside—got paid fer shootin' 'em in the
back—an' it didn't bother him none. But y' shoulda
heard him with the croaker. 'Doctor, doctor,' he used
t' howl, 'please don't lemme die! I'm too young to
die! Get aholda my people an' they'll pay you plenty.
Get aholda some outside specialists. Save me!' My
God, it was awful—him that'd bumped off them guys
without givin' 'em any kind of a break at all."

"Did he die?"

"Sure. Who the hell ever comes back from that
hospital if they's anything really wrong with 'em? . . .
I had pretty good luck when I was up there that time.
Humphreys had a lotta good stuff, an' I got most of it
before them thievin' nurses could get t' his cot an' strip
him. . . . I rated a drag with Jimmy, the night nurse
in the ward. He was a swell guy. Sixty-two years
old an' had served over forty of 'em in different stirs.
God, but that guy knew how t' do time. Nothin'
bothered him. He gimme Humphreys' junk—most
of it—an' you shoulda heard them day nurses howl
when they showed up fer work the next morning!"

He points to his "Sunday" shoes. "These dogs was Humphreys'. Good ones, too. I had 'em fer over three years an' they ain't even started to wear out yet."

"You dirty ghoul!" I cry. "Out stripping corpses!"

"Baloney!" says Red, grinning. "You oughta see them day nurses if you wanta see some real ghouls at work. A guy ain't no more'n took his final breath before they're swarming all over him like a pack of hungry lions on a pile of meat. They strip him right down to his last shoelace. No kidding—I've seen them guys knock the gold outta a stiff's teeth. And once when a one-legged guy died, that scurvy head nurse swiped his leg and sold it to another one-legged guy that'd just busted his."

That night, Mac stops at my cell when he is making the rounds with the first light for a smoke. He balances his carbide lamp on one of the crossbars, eyes me seriously, and asks, "Listen, have you been tangling with Carlisle again?"

"Yes. We had a little run-in this afternoon in the yard. Why?"

He puts his lips close to the bars and motions me near, so no one will hear him.

"Remember," he whispers, "I haven't said a word. But here's a tip. Carlisle just asked me to tell the deputy that a certain party in the cell hall had something hidden in his cell."

"Red?" I whisper in fright.

Mac looks at me scornfully. "No, not Red."

A wave of cold suddenly passes along my spine.

"Oh."

"The deputy'll be up here pretty quick to shake down that party's cell. I don't think he's the kind of a guy that'd hide things in his cell, so I'd hate to see him go to the hole and then D.W. for the rest of his time."

My heart is pounding fast. "What's hidden? Where is it?"

"If this party'd look under his pillow, or his mattress, or see if it's hanging on a string down the ventilator shaft, he might find it."

"What'll he do with it?"

"I don't know. But whatever he does, once he's picked it up, I'd advise him not to get rid of it before he wipes his fingerprints from it."

"If it'll hold a print, why not just leave it as it is, so the deputy can find out who had it in the first place?"

Mac snaps back suddenly from the bars, looks at me in amazement, then says in a normal voice, "By God, Ross, you've surer'n hell got something there. . . ." His voice again drops to a whisper. "I've got to report this, you know. Mean my job if I didn't and the deputy found out about it, which he would. . . . Get ready."

He passes down the gallery to report to Armstrong. I start carefully searching the cell. And then, tied with string to the under frame of my cot—out of sight, but insured against falling—I find it. A long, homemade knife, fashioned from a file or a piece of steel—such as might be found in the blacksmith shop, where a weapon like this could be made without a great deal of danger of being discovered.

I leave the knife just as I found it, but turn back the thin mattress and the blankets so the deputy will realize I know it's there and will think I'm waiting to report it to the night officer when he comes by with the next light.

I sit on my chair and wait. . . . Carlisle has evidently decided he'll put me out of circulation for keeps. For if this knife had been found on me, I'd not only have gone to the hole: the knife itself would have been evidence enough to put me in the detention ward, where dangerous prisoners are kept for the duration of their sentences. D.W. is on the opposite side of the hole, in the same building, and is a sort of glorified solitary confinement, where the inmate is locked up all the time, but retains his reading, writing, mail and tobacco privileges. . . .

Good old Mac. If all the guards were just one-tenth as white as he, prison would be almost endurable.

Carlisle! But how, I ask myself, could he get the knife into my cell? It's almost impossible for a shop inmate to roam around the cell halls. An officer is always on duty. . . . Still, it's not absolutely impossible. The guard might have been busy this afternoon. Carlisle might possibly have sneaked in and, on a one hundred to one chance, got away with it. I try to satisfy my mind with this solution, but it rings far from true, for, here in Stony Point, no one outside his cell is ever absolutely free from observation.

A horrible thought hits me: What if there are no fingerprints on the knife? Ow!

But it's not too late. I can still untie it and throw it down the ventilator shaft. Maybe the deputy won't have the bottom of the shaft opened and searched. I could wipe out the prints I leave on it, and they'd never be able absolutely to hang it on me.

Nuts! It'd be just another thing for the parole board to bring up. Besides, how could Carlisle tie it up there without leaving at least a portion of one print?

I make up my mind. No more monkey business for me. I've been in enough trouble already. The knife stays where it is.

In a few minutes, I hear the deputy and Mac running up the stairs. . . . I can imagine Carlisle, sitting gloating in his cell, ears to the bars, waiting for the sounds that will tell him I'm going out of circulation permanently, his beady little eyes darting back and forth, his tongue wetting his slit of mouth, his pasty face unnaturally flushed.

Then the drop-bar is thrown, and two pairs of footsteps pad down the gallery. I stand up to the bars and wait for them. The deputy seems a bit surprised to find me as I am. His eyes pop a little when he sees the mattress thrown back.

"Deputy," I say, "I was just going to send for you the next time the officer came by. Some dirty rat planted a knife in my bed."

"Where is it?" asks the deputy, at the same time, in an aside, asking Mac for the key.

"Right there, under the framework, tied out of sight with that string."

"How'd you find it if it's out of sight?"

"I was going to turn the mattress when I saw the string."

"Take the knife down and hand it through the bars to the officer before I come in."

"No, wait! There'll be fingerprints on it. You can bring them out if I don't touch it. Then we'll know who was trying to frame me."

The deputy's eyebrows raise. "By golly, you're right. Here—" he hands me his pen-knife "—cut the strings and let the thing fall in your handkerchief."

I do as he directs, then hand the homemade shiv, the pen-knife and the handkerchief to him through the bars.

"Okay." He unlocks my cell. "Come on, Ross. I hope for your sake you guessed right on this."

We walk down the corridor, past Carlisle's cell. He grins evilly, and draws his fingers across his throat. Then we pass Red's cell. The hairy man is at the bars, his face looking troubled. I wink as we pass.

In the Bertillon room, an inmate is rousted from his cot, where he is reading. Armstrong says,

"Here, bring out any prints you find on this."

The Bertillon man pulls on his pants and goes to work. I sit down. The deputy stands with the finger-print expert. . . . I think—pretty soft for the Bertillon man. He sleeps right in his office, eats officers' food, can have matches in the office, and gets about a dollar a day. He's a robber serving forty years, and should have quite a roll saved up when he goes out. . . . Some inmates, who make only thirty-five cents a day, go out of here with several hundred dollars—and get rolled for it the first night!

The deputy and the Bertillon man bend over the table, and I see the latter counting whorls. Then he steps to the files and brings out two sets of cards.

"One," he announces, and my heart stops while I listen, "is Carlisle, 100,888. The other is Wolf, 100,544."

The deputy smiles. "That clears you, Ross."

I heave a sigh of relief. "Yessir."

"You and Carlisle still having run-ins?"

"Yes, he thinks I framed him into the hole on that soda rap."

"Did you?"

"Hell, no! Wouldn't I look swell, framing somebody on something, when I'm squawking all the time about being in here on a frame, myself?"

The deputy steps into the anteroom and tells the night captain to bring Carlisle and the Wolf from their cells.

"The Wolf," I think. So that was the connection. Carlisle used him the same way Red and Dale and Pat used Billie.

The pair enter, looking badly frightened.

Armstrong barks, "I don't suppose you men know why you're here?"

The pair shake their heads.

"Which one of you planted that knife in Ross's cell—you?"   He levels his finger at Carlisle.

"No, no," cries the white-faced man.   "I didn't do it.   I don't know nothing about it.   He's the guy that's always trying to frame me."

"Then what are your fingerprints doing on it?" asks the deputy.

Carlisle's eyes bug out.   He seeks to hide behind a lie.

"I sold it to Wolf.   He bought it from me for a pair of shoes.   He wanted to frame Ross, but I wouldn't go for it, and wouldn't let him have it till he promised not to."

The Wolf starts to blow up, but Armstrong says, "What about you?   Your fingerprints are on here, and Ross's aren't."

"I'll admit what I did," cries the Wolf, "but I ain't taking that rat's raps too.   He gimme a pair of shoes for planting the knife in Ross's cell.   He told me Ross was out to get him, and that was the only way he'd be safe."

Carlisle starts screaming to high heaven, but the deputy and the night captain grab the pair and lead them off to the hole.

18

THE days and weeks now tramp by without variation. Seldom does anything occur to make one day
stand out from the rest. No word from Stacey; he
is evidently still in hiding. No word from Lockhart;
he has returned to his headquarters in the East. A
letter from Joyce each night, telling me over and over
of her hopes and fears, but trying always to buoy me
up and keep my courage at a high point. She visits
me each month and is always certain that my release
lies just a few days ahead, but her eyes are losing their
luster, and shadows now add to the darkness beneath
her lashes. The continued silence is sapping my
strength. And the suspense is undermining Joyce's
health. We are baffled at the apparent inactivity of
Lockhart and Stacey.

If the attorney had never called on either Joyce or
me—if Stacey had flown from the courtroom and
vanished without any effort to get in touch with us—
I could believe that the ex-bank-robber had merely
made good his escape and forgotten about me, once
he was free. I could believe all that Red feels is so
certain about Stacey. . . . But I talked with him that
day in the shop; I know he meant every word he said—
that there is honor among thieves. And, as soon as he
was free, not only did he get in touch with Joyce; he

also sent his attorney to me. There are only two things left for me to believe: either that something has arisen over which he has no control, or that both Stacey and Lockhart, like many of the others who have sought to help me, ran into the same veil of secrecy and ignorance which surrounds my case, and, not having the heart to tell me the whole thing is hopeless, quietly gave up.

Our hours of recreation in the prison yard are over until the snow leaves the ground. The poplar trees outside the north wall are bare as my hopes. All is work and silence in Stony Point, for we are given no Saturday afternoon of recreation during the winter months. On holiday mornings only, we will be granted an hour's freedom in the corridors of the cell halls, but only five such hours lie between now and next spring—five hours in which to talk and pace the floor like lost souls and try, for a moment, to forget that we are where we are.

Sunday. The editor of the prison paper is sick in his cell and sent word via the deputy for me to go to church and cover the sermon. It will be my first time to attend chapel service here.

We march in to the music of the band. A woman soloist, accompanied by a young girl at the piano, sings a hymn. As she stands piously on the stage, the eyes of the inmates undress her. There are three large chairs behind a portable altar. She takes refuge in the one that partially hides her from the inmates. Evidently

she realizes why half of them attend church. . . .
She looks a little frightened and ill at ease, there
on the stage of the auditorium-chapel, with a thousand
pairs of woman-hungry eyes focused on her.   I can't
help but feel sorry for her.   She means well.

The chaplain is a pulpit-thumper.   He rages and
roars, preaches hell-fire and brimstone.   He is an
actor—an orator, with the power to hold his audience.
And he realizes his power—wields it over the inmates
who take their religion too seriously.   He builds up
his sermon to a crashing finale, striding across the
stage, arms outstretched, calling on God and Jesus to
save these wayward children. . . . The men blink and
stare at their shoes.   The fanatics weep unashamedly.
The chaplain calls for all who wish to be saved to raise
their hands.   A smattering of fingers reach upward.
The other inmates glance sheepishly at one another and
then resume their inspection of their shoes. . . . A
long, droning prayer rolls into eternity, and at last the
sermon is ended.

Then something unusual is happening.   An inmate
is struggling to rise.   His neighbors try to hold him
in his seat, but he breaks from them and dashes into
the aisle.

He screams, "Fathah, fathah, save me, save me!
Lemme kiss yo' hand!"

He rushes down the aisle, bowling over the guards
who try to stop him.   He scrambles into the pit,
clambers to the top of the piano, and leaps onto the
stage.   The chaplain is horror-stricken.   The inmate

flings himself to the floor, kissing the preacher's feet and snatching at his hands. Deputy Armstrong and two officers rush to the stage and grab the inmate. They pull him erect. It is Mose, the Negro swamper.

Mose isn't doing time any more; his release from the stark horror of prison is already complete.

He starts screaming, "Save me, fathah, save me! They put poison in my tobacco, an' every night they leave the black bottle on my shelf!"

The officers drag him away. We hear his screams from backstage. The band blares out, but, as we march back to our cells, I hear only the cries of Mose, the colored boy who got religion and couldn't handle it.

Christmas: Last night Mac gave you a tailor-made cigarette and two cookies, then stood guard while you ate the cookies and smoked the cigarette. Then, just as a joke—the kind of joke that sometimes turns around and hits you in the eye—you hung your sock on one of the crossbars of your cell. And in the morning, there was an orange in it.

New Year: At midnight, the whistles woke you. All the locomotives in the railway yard at the county seat, all the bells in the town, all the auto horns, all the guns, everything and everyone in the whole world joyously whistled and rang and honked and banged and shouted and yelled. And you sat on your cot and wondered what had happened to Stacey and Lockhart.

Lincoln's birthday—Washington's birthday: Pie on

the table twice in one month. . . . This life—so precious.

March: The wind booms in the sky, and the clouds race to the horizon, and rain falls on the snow, and one brave robin lifts his voice as the world stirs with returning life.

And your blood stirs too, and you feel tiny prickles between your shoulder blades when you remember that next month you go to the board—that next week you'll be given a preliminary interview by the parole agent. . . . You try not to dwell upon it all too much. It's a little bit frightening, after all the long months of work and silence—you're afraid to think of actually going out into a free world again.

Red and I stand at the window of the crowded corridor and look out upon a scum of dirty snow.

"Good Friday," I say.

"What's good about it?" growls Red.

"At times, I think you've actually got possibilities."

"Whatcha mean?"

"Nothing. Skip it."

"You're nuts."

We stumble along the corridor. I wait momentarily while Red places a quick bet on a prize fight to be held next week. When he rejoins me, he mutters, "I got a new Herman. We'll make some dough framing up roach races."

"Catch a few for reserves."

Dale, Johnny Carr and Pat O'Brien signal us.

Dale looks all around, then says in a muffled voice, "We're about ready to crash the joint now. Everything's set like I told you before."

Red says, "When do we leave?"

"Sometime next month."

I ask, "Who all's in on it?"

"Not very many yet. We're watching our step. Just Pat and Johnny and me and six or seven others— Seiver and Elman and Lewis from the wood shop."

I say, "You must be nuts. You'll never make it."

"That's what you think," says Dale. "We'll make it—or else."

"It's suicide," I say. "Nobody's ever gone over these walls or out these gates."

"That's no sign we can't," says Dale.

"There're a million guns in the arsenal. You'll all get killed."

"What if we do?" says Johnny Carr. "We've all got the book, and we'd as soon be dead as in here any longer anyway."

"The hell with that talk," says Dale. "We're going out; the screws go to the morgue. We'll have plenty of guns to take care of them." His eyes snap and he grits his teeth.

"Where'll you get 'em?" I ask.

"That guy that's going out April second's gonna take care of everything."

"But how'll you get the guns past the gates?"

"A truck'll come down for a load of twine. The driver'll leave the rods and shells with a trusty on the loading platform of the outside warehouse."

"But how'll you get the guns through? All the trusties are searched every night when they come in."

Dale snorts. "That's the easiest part of it. All the trusty's gotta do is stick 'em in a carload of lumber outside the walls. Then when the car comes inside to be unloaded, the boys from the wood shop'll hide the gats and the shells in the sawdust bins till we need 'em. . . . I'll get yours and Red's and slip 'em to you. We'll be out in the yard again by that time."

"Mine and Red's!" I cry. "Don't come fooling around us with any guns! We're not in on this. I had enough trouble over that Stacey mess."

"Don't tell me you're backing out now! My God, we were all figuring on you."

"Backing out! This's the first time I've even heard of it since last year."

Red says, "I'm up to the board next week; if they don't gimme a break, I'm in."

"And I'm up to the board next month, but don't figure on me," I say, "even if I do get continued."

Dale says, "Better figure on coming along, Ross. That parole board ain't gonna do anything for you. They ain't giving anybody a break—especially a guy that's in as bad as you."

"I can't help it. Count me out."

Several other inmates start horning in on the party, so we break it up.

"And don't fergit to count me in," says Red.

We move on down the corridor.

"What's the matter with you, Red?" I demand. "Have you lost your mind?"

"No, but I'm plenty fed up on doing time in this nut house. If that board don't gimme a break, I'm gonna lam with 'em."

"But it's just like committing suicide. I don't want to see you killed or locked up for the rest of your life for killing one of these screws. And that's what you'll get, no matter who shoots him, as long as you're in on it—life in the hole, at that. You haven't got a chance of beating this joint. That wall's thirty feet high."

"Nobody's gotta go over it if he's got a gat in his mitt." Red warms up to the subject. "We'll wheel outta this joint like a dose of salts through a tall Swede—right out the gates, by God, I'll betcha. And jest let one of them dirty screws git in my way——"

"But, Red——"

The bell rings. The holiday is over. The bountiful Warden Tang's silent system will now reign for another month or so, for we get no holiday on Easter Sunday—no holiday at all now until the snow is gone, and we can go into the yard on Saturday afternoons.

Four days later, I find the letter on my cot when I return for the night. It is from Joyce. I scorch the paper with my pipe. As the words take form, the last of my hope drains from me like blood oozing from a torn vein.

A.P. reports Stacey captured in Los Angeles today following a bank robbery. He says he'll
fight extradition. Lockhart 'phoned long distance
from New York. He's leaving for California at
once, but says not to lose hope. Stacey was working on something just before his capture. I'll be
down to see you before you go to the board.

I slowly tear the letter into tiny bits, flush them
down the toilet, flop down on my chair, and rest my
head in my hands. Mac stops in front of my cell.

"What's wrong? You weren't up to the board today, were you?"

I shake my head. "Not till next month."

"Then what you feeling so low about? You
haven't got a denial yet."

"Mac, I hear Stacey was captured."

"How'd you hear that? It just happened yesterday, and I didn't know it till I saw the paper this
morning."

"I heard a rumor."

"Well, his capture won't hurt you any. That
Stacey business is all done and forgotten."

I shrug. "I guess so. . . . Tell me, Mac. Red
went up to the board today. What did he get?"

"That's what I stopped for. I just gave him his
slip. . . . They continued his case a year."

A chill seizes me. "God, and he's been here eight
years."

"For stealing a tire," supplements Mac.

"What'll they do to me? I thought I might get off
with four or five months if I didn't make a parole;

now I suppose I'll be lucky if I don't get more than a year."

"Couple of the boys that went up for the first time got five years apiece today.   And that little guy in the print shop got three. . . . The board's only given eight paroles so far—out of about fifty applications."

"They're getting tougher all the time. . . . With the new men pouring in the way they are, where's the deputy going to keep everybody?"

Mac sets his carbide torch on one of the crossbars.

"You got me.   Joint's so jammed now we can hardly squeeze another cot in the corridors. . . . Damn near every cell's occupied."

"How'd the boys take their setbacks from the board?"

"Red didn't give a damn.   That guy knows how to do time.   But the other boys felt pretty bad.   They've all been moved down on the first floor so they can't jump overboard in the morning."

"How come the deputy started that?"

Mac shrugs.   "The suicide rate was getting pretty high for a while.   Hardly a month went by that somebody who'd been turned down for a long time didn't jump over the rail."

He picks up his torch and walks on down the gallery.

I sit on my cot and try to think, but my mind is a giant kaleidoscope that flashes tiny, unrecognizable pictures of a chaotic life: Stacey in the Los Angeles jail, charged with bank robbery, and possibly holding my entire future in the palm of his hands; the board room, with Grayce peering at me again, as he did in the courtroom during my trial; men moving from the fourth gallery to the first; Fargo Red involved in a bloody riot; Joyce crying when she receives word of the outcome of my interview with the parole board. . . . Ahead of me stretches a future as black as a clouded, midnight sky. I fall back on my cot and close my eyes.

19

MAD DOG Mooney signals that he has a pass for me. It is to see Harkness, the parole agent. I change my clothes and trek to the anteroom of the deputy's office. Seven or eight inmates are lined up ahead of me—men who have served more time than I but who are seeing the parole board for the first time next month. We face the wall as we wait for our names to be called. The wait is not long, for there is little to tell the agent beyond our intentions if we are freed and any extenuating circumstances that surround our imprisonment.

Harkness calls me. I step to his desk. He smiles absently, shuffles through his folders for my file, and motions me to sit down.

"You want to see the board?" he asks.

"Of course."

"Some of the men don't, you know—the short-timers."

I nod. "Well, I do. I'm certainly not a short-timer."

He questions me concerning my past—my relatives, my schooling, my former jobs.

"Figure on going home to your mother if you're paroled?" he asks.

"Yes."

"Got a job lined up?"

231

"Oh, sure. I can go back to work for the paper."

"Not while you're on parole."

"Why not?"

"Paroled men can't have jobs that keep them out after nine o'clock at night."

"But the newspaper business is all I know."

"Can't help it. If you're released, you'll have to have another job lined up first."

Bill and Lew and Joe—they should be able to find something in another line for me while I'm on parole.

I ask, "Do you think I'll get a parole?"

"Well, that's up to the board. I don't have anything to say about it. But I don't like to kid you guys along and make you think you're going to get something when chances are you might be given a setback. . . . In your case, I couldn't say. You still maintain you're not guilty, and the board's liable to take that as an indication you're not punished enough yet. They figure that every man's guilty and should admit it and show a desire to start all over with a clean slate. If he's not guilty, the board figures the pardon board would have released him. . . . And you've already been denied by the pardon board."

"But, my God, they can't want a man to admit something if it isn't true. I didn't kill those people. Somebody ran that car into the other one after I'd been slugged and framed with a lot of whiskey in my car. Somebody headed it down the road when the other car was coming, then jumped out and left me to take the rap."

"Well, it isn't only that, Ross. You've got that Stacey escape chalked up against you too. We haven't any proof, but we know you were implicated in it some way. The parole board has a record of that. And this is only your first time up to the board. They seldom turn out a man on the first interview unless he's from out of the state and will take a conditional discharge and not come back into the state till after his maximum sentence expires."

"I'll do that," I offer.

"The board can't do that with residents of this state. We can't be dumping our criminals off on some other states; all we can do is send them back their own criminals as fast as we can release them."

"There isn't much chance for me then?"

"I won't say for sure, but the way it looks to me, you may get continued for a little while—maybe six months or a year."

My stomach suddenly feels as if the bottom of it has been gnawed away. A chill touches my spine and a numbness creeps into my brain. But this is what I've been telling myself all along—trying to steel myself against when it comes—so I won't be too overwhelmed at a six months' or year's denial from the parole board. But in the back of my mind has always ticked the hope that the board will do something unexpected and release me the first time up. Even in spite of the agent's forecast, the hope is still there, ticking furiously now, in an attempt to defeat the wave of futility that has swept over me.

I leave the office and return to the shop.   Hunter is just going out on a pass.   I'll have to work alone with Red until Hunter returns.   Double labor again.

Squires is on the stand.   When I return the initialed pass, he asks, "How's it look?"

I shake my head.   "Not so hot."

Squires is a nice young fellow.   He says, "Don't let it get you down, Ross.   After all, Harkness is only the agent.   He doesn't know for sure what's going to be done.   He only guesses."

"Thanks, but I'm afraid he has a pretty good idea. He doesn't use any idle words and has a reason for everything he says."

"Well, hang on and keep your nose clean.   Maybe things won't turn out as bad as you think."

Red raises his eyebrows when I return to the machine.   Surreptitiously I point my thumb down.   Red makes off he's holding a pistol and grins. . . . Still determined, now that he's been denied for a year, to go through with the riot.

The morning passes.   A runner from the deputy's office brings Mooney, who has returned to the stand, a transfer slip.   Then the officer sends Johnny Carr over to take Hunter's place on our machine.

Squires is standing at the rear of the shop.   I slide back there, take a bale knife from the rack, and start opening sisal.   Squires walks over beside me.

"What'd they do with Hunter?" I ask.   "Give him a clerk's job?"

"Why, is he gone?"

I point to Carr.

"I'll go see," says Squires.

In a moment he is back.

"He went out. His attorney appealed and got him another trial on new evidence."

"That looks pretty good for him, doesn't it?" I didn't know Hunter very well and am a bit overwhelmed at the suddenness of things.

"Pretty good?" says Squires, smiling. "It couldn't be much better. Nobody's ever come back that was granted a new trial. As a rule they aren't even prosecuted."

"That's what they're trying to get me—another trial on new evidence."

"They're waiting long enough. You've only got two years in which to file."

"That's what I've been thinking."

The daily letter from Joyce is in my cell. The paper has lost the first of its lawsuits over the story which led to my imprisonment. A notice of appeal has been filed, and the cases may drag out for a while yet. . . . It's just like telling me that as long as they're hanging fire, the parole board won't think of releasing me—not with Grayce as chairman of the board.

Now my nights are black misery. For hours I lie thinking of my pending interview with the board of parole. I try to decide what I shall do when I am actually in the board's room. I remember all the advice I've been given by inmates who have seen the board three, four and five times. Some have said, "Don't say anything at all. Just answer their questions and get out. Don't antagonize them by talking too much." Others have said, "Tear right into them. Give them both barrels and let them know you deserve a parole." And still others have contended, "Don't even go in to see the board. Your case is already decided and it doesn't do any good to go in there. They'll just try to make you sore and blow up. . . . They won't let you out till they're good and ready anyway."

The board is especially hard on men who are residents of this state. Out-of-state men, as Harkness said, are sometimes released after serving a minimum amount of time and have no strings attached to their release, save that they must remain out of this state until their maximum sentences have expired. But the home guards are kept in the prison year after year, having their applications denied again and again. And then when they are finally freed, they are kept under the strictest surveillance for the balance of their terms. Even such slight infractions of the parole rules as staying out after nine o'clock or drinking one glass of beer means years of additional imprisonment, for parole violators are shunted right back to Stony Point without a hearing. . . . And if I am paroled, my maximum sentence is twenty years.

The visit with Joyce is not gay.
I ask, "What have you heard?"

Joyce opens the collar of her gray tweed coat. The day is warm and spring-like—one of those late March days that sometimes precede a blizzard.

"He's fighting extradition. We're having Ray Pick follow up the case. I'm afraid he's coming back."

"Have you heard anything from Lockhart?"

"Yes. That's why I came down today. Your friend had already located Limpy."

My heart bounds. The guard looks at us quizzically, trying to figure out what we're talking about.

"Did—" the question is hard to ask "—did he learn anything?"

"He got in trouble before Lockhart could talk to him, but the attorney has some helpers who will see him before what's-his-name comes back."

I squeeze Joyce's hand. "Maybe everything isn't as black as it looks then."

"Listen, lady," says the guard. "You'll have to speak right up. No secret conversations allowed."

Rules again——

"Have you been able to do anything with the parole board?"

Joyce's face reflects her fear, and her eyes are troubled.

"We're doing everything we possibly can. All the boys in the office have called on the Governor."

"How about Grayce—has anyone seen him?"

"Yes, just about everyone in the city that amounts to anything, but he always says the same thing: it's up to the other members of the board as much as himself—that they'll consider your case fairly. As for Grayce—he's never yet promised anything good, and the other members won't commit themselves."

"That guy's got a nerve talking about considering anything fairly. He knows why I'm in here, and he'll give me the same medicine he passed out to some of the other boys this month. . . . You should see some of the denial slips that came out of the board room at the last meeting. Some of them were for as much as five years. . . . I've mentioned my friend Fargo Red in my letters—well, he's got in eight years for stealing a tire, and the board gave him a continuance of another year. When that's up, they may give him the rest of his sentence."

Joyce's face pales. Her fear breaks down her natural reserve. "Oh, my darling. They couldn't treat you like that. I'd die. I wouldn't want to live any more if you weren't coming home soon."

"Well, we'll know before long—just a little over two weeks. . . . The next time I see you, it'll be settled."

"You're so melancholy today, Frank. Can't you try to cheer up? It isn't that it harms only you; it hurts me too."

"I'm sorry, dear. I've been here over a year. I've been thrown in the hole and subjected to almost everything a man doesn't even want to think about. I'm wasting my life in here for something I didn't do. . . . Sometimes it gets me down—especially now, when my last chance is probably shot. I'm feeling low today, but I'll snap out of it and be all right."

I wish I could tell her about the impending riot—another beat lies in the offing for the paper, but I'll have to chance the lemon juice again. . . . If the boys really do make good their attempt to escape, the paper couldn't want a sweeter scoop than a picture of them boiling out the door or over the wall. But first I'll have to find out the exact date. And then maybe there won't be time to write.

The guard touches my knee. Visit over. Mentally I kick myself for my ugly frame of mind.

"I'll be praying and hoping every minute," breathes Joyce. "And your mother'll be praying and hoping too. She's just about frantic, but we've kept her from making another trip down here. The last one was too hard on her. . . . And you told her once you wouldn't take a parole even if they'd give you one because it would look as though you were admitting your guilt. She worries continually about that."

"That was a long time ago. I'll take anything at all—anything, just to get out of here."

The guard says, "Your time's up."

I draw Joyce close to me.

She whispers, "Be brave, Frank. And remember that regardless of how things come out, I'll always love you and be waiting for you."

I stumble back to the shops.

20

THIS morning when the bell rang for us to go to breakfast, I thought, "Maybe you're hearing this for the last time." When I sat down in the dining hall, I told myself, "This may be your last meal in prison." For the parole board has arrived to interview the April applicants. And, though the board generally sits for three days, I'll be one of the first inmates interviewed, for I've been here a long time. Squires told me that my serial number was seventh on the list. And seven is supposed to be a lucky number.

The morning has dragged interminably. The time is only ten o'clock. I have been working like a madman, trying to keep my addled mind off thoughts of what may lie ahead—I imagine terrible things. I have piled one set of twine fiber into ten three-hundred-pound bales—fifty-five minutes of back-breaking labor, but the work didn't tire me a bit. I am jumpy and over-anxious for the interview for which I have waited over a year. Now Red is piling bales, and as fast as he finishes them I drag them from the box, weigh them so we'll keep the average at three hundred pounds, and slam them over beside the machine which will next process them. Johnny Carr just tags along as I try to tire myself into forgetting that this is the biggest day of my life.

Then Red starts smiling and nods toward Squires. I wheel around. Squires waves a pass. I change my clothes. The pass summons me to the board room.

"Better start praying," says Squires. "I hear Grayce was on a bender last night and he's pretty tough."

"You're a lot of help."

"Good luck, Ross."

I have no memory of walking from the shop to the gates, but I find myself lined up with six others just outside the mail room. Sand is sprinkled on the floor, as is the invariable custom. I scuff at it with my feet and am warned by the turnkey to stand quietly. I lean against the bricks of the wall and close my eyes. Again I am admonished—this time to stand erect with folded arms. The other inmates chuckle. I shift my feet. The minutes drag slowly past.

Then the turnkey opens the gate and we are herded into the mail room. Chairs are strung along the wall, where we are permitted to sit and wait our turn with the board. Two inmate clerks work at high book-keepers' desks. Officers Hultman and Klein sit at a long, low table just outside the entrance to the parole board's office, censoring all incoming mail.

I sink into my chair and strive for nonchalance. But my mouth is dry, my heart heavy, and my hands stickily wet. I find myself yawning repeatedly and recall my yawns in the courtroom while I waited for Stacey and Garsky to strike.

The first inmate of our group is called by Harkness, and enters the parole room. We all move up a notch in the chairs. Even in the mail room, there is white sand on the floor. With the points of my shoes, I pack it into tiny mounds. Then I smooth it out and make imprints of my feet, as I used to do in the snow when I was a kid.

Ten minutes slip by, an old-fashioned clock banging out the seconds. The door of the board room opens, and the first inmate comes out. His face is wet and white, and his lips twitch. He must have got a bawling out—a good sign, according to inmates who have been interviewed before, for the board wastes no time lecturing an inmate they intend to deny a parole. And he was in there ten minutes. Somebody once told me something about the average length of time if a man was going to be released. . . . I'll time myself when I go in and when I come out. If I remember.

And now six men have passed into the board room, and I am next. When the last man comes out, I shall enter the room and make my bid for freedom. I have waited over a year for this.

Another group of inmates is shunted into the mail room. They look scared, and shuffle their feet, and gaze sadly at their shoes. The hands of some of them tremble. Mentally they are trying to rehearse their pleas to the board—trying to remember all they planned to say.

The door opens. The last inmate leaves the board room. He is cursing beneath his breath. His face is white and taut. The turnkey initials his pass and sends him back to work.

The seconds tick slowly on. I watch the clock. The board has been studying for five minutes. A long time. And maybe they're reviewing my case—or at least they may have spent half the time on mine and the other half on the man who just came out. Two and a half minutes. That's a good sign. Or is it? I can't remember what I've been told.

Then the door opens and Harkness sticks his head into the mail room.

"Ross."

I rise, and then suddenly I am in the board room, facing Grayce, the chairman, who helped prosecute my case.

Grayce sits at the head of the table. He glances at me cursorily and orders me to sit down, indicating a chair on his left. I perch gingerly on the seat, grasp the arms, and try to swallow the balls of cotton in my mouth.

"How are you feeling?" asks the chairman.

The set routine. Every inmate is asked the same question. It is never varied and means nothing. I have heard it over and over again from other inmates.

"I'm pretty well."

"And you're the man who gets drunk and kills innocent people with his car, are you?"

I had made up my mind to be submissive, but the chairman is evidently looking for trouble—trying to make me blow up.

"I guess you know me," I mutter. "You helped prosecute me."

"Feeling a little troublesome this morning, are you? That isn't the proper attitude to take with the board. After all, we're here to release men who feel properly penitent and show a desire to lead a decent life in the future."

"I've never led any other kind of life. I guess you know that well enough."

"All we know is what is a matter of record. Is it still your contention that you're innocent?"

"It certainly is."

"Then you can't have any use for the parole board. We're interested only in men who acknowledge their guilt and want to atone for their wrongs."

"I've been to the pardon board. They won't do a thing for me. I thought that if you'd let me out, I might be able to find who framed me. . . . I've certainly served enough time for something I didn't do."

"The pardon board doesn't feel that you're innocent."

"What do you want me to do," I cry, "confess to a crime I didn't commit? I'll stay here the whole twenty years before I do that."

The chairman is as smooth as oil. "The main trouble with you, Ross, is you're too self-pitying. You'll go to any end to accomplish your purpose, if you believe you're being abused or mistreated."

"That's not true. I'm in here on a bum rap, and any man in the world in my position would take the stand I'm taking."

"If it's not true, why did you help Stacey to escape?"

I shake my head. No lies now. And I can see there's not much use in making any plea. The words which I intended to speak are stuck in the back of my throat. I am overcome with the futility of trying to explain anything. If it hadn't been the Stacey mess, Grayce would have thought up something else. . . . So I clasp my hands together and hope.

"You haven't been a very good example for the rest of the inmates," continues Grayce, "and it might not be the proper thing to turn you loose on a defenseless society just yet. You don't seem properly impressed with the reason for your imprisonment. You've got to realize that you can't get drunk and drive around killing people. It's murder, as your admirable ex-newspaper once pointed out, just as surely as if you used a loaded gun. . . . Then there's the matter of aiding Stacey in making an escape—oh, don't deny it. It's as plain as the nose on your face. Too much pressure on your behalf has been brought to bear since Stacey escaped—pressure from a source other than the kind your old newspaper would use—has used, in fact."

What can I say? How can I explain my helping Stacey, when I'm not sure myself why I did it, other than that I wanted to halt this undeserved punishment? How can I make him understand that no decent person can snitch on a fellow inmate, no matter how serious the consequences of the other's act may be? There is nothing for me to do but sit there and take it.

"Well," says the chairman, "have you anything to say to the board?"

"I'll appreciate anything you can do for me."

Another member asks, "Do you go to church regularly?"

"Just once in a great while."

"Why not? Don't you think that, in your position especially, you need divine guidance?"

"No. When I go to church, it's for the prison paper. I quit believing in God and church long ago."

His eyes pop open. "What!"

"God hasn't been giving me any breaks during the past year or so. If He wants me to believe in Him, it's His move now."

"But you should have faith in God, my boy. He'll see you through every hardship."

"I guess I'll keep what little faith I've got left in the pardon board and the parole board. They can turn me out of here, not God, and I want to go home."

He closes his mouth with a snap. The chairman hurriedly says, "We'll see what we can do for you."

I really must be a little bit crazy, for I realize that I'd never have said what I did if I were normal. The months of imprisonment put those words in my mouth, and they were spoken without conscious effort on my part.

Then the back part of my numb mind tells me that nothing has been said about my obtaining work when I am freed, and I realize the board isn't even interested in questioning me about it. And I break and start to make a desperate plea, hoping to convince them that I should be released, but knowing in my heart that any plea I make is useless.

I begin to talk, but Grayce irritably cuts me short. He repeats, "We'll see what we can do." Already he is turning to the next folder—the case of the inmate who waits next in line outside the door, as I did, in an alternating state of hope and despair.

I open the door, hand my pass to the turnkey and wait for him to initial it and unlock the gate. My eyes fall on the clock. I was in the board room less than seven minutes. . . . I waited over a year for a seven-minute interview.

The gate opens. I start through it, but the captain of the solitary and a small, slight man in civilian clothes pass through ahead of me. He turns his face to mine.

Stacey!

God in Heaven! This is the end of Frank Ross.

I follow the pair down the long hall. They turn in at the deputy's office and go directly into the solitary. The solid steel door clangs shut. . . .

I stumble down the steps, cross the yard and enter the shop. Squires says something, but I float back to the breaker. Red signals me. I turn my thumbs down. He takes a desperate chance and whispers hurriedly, "We'll lam outta here together."

I look at the clock. Almost noon. Hours and hours until six o'clock when the slips are passed around. But I haven't much doubt of what I'll get. Six months.

Or possibly a year. Or even eighteen months. . . .
The last thought is like a trip hammer smashing
against my throbbing head. My mind blurs. . . .
Eighteen months. Could they possibly continue my
case for eighteen months? Could I go on living in
here for eighteen more long months? . . . I try to
think of the lifers who have been here thirty-five and
forty years. But the thought does me no good. They
are who they are, and I am who I am. Nothing can
ever change that. My troubles overshadow any others
because they affect me. . . . Eighteen months . . .
Stacey, what happened?

The day passes in a succession of unremembered
blurs. Then at last the supper bell rings and I peck at
my meal. It is poor fare—beans and bread and black
chicory. I swallow only a mouthful. When the
guard orders me to finish what I have left on my plate,
I plead illness. He says nothing, but moves back to
his position.

At last, the marching bell sounds, and we rise and
file from the dining hall. Down the arcade, into the
north cell hall, and up the steps. I slam the cell door
and stand with my hand on the bars, waiting for the
count to be made. As my friends pass, they mutter,
"Whaddja make?" I point my thumb down. They
shake their heads.

The screws dash past, double-locking us with keys.
They count us, make a mistake, and count us again.
At last the gong clangs.

I move to the rear of my cell, take off my coat, wash
my hands and face. . . . And all the time my mind is
saying, "The slips'll be around at six." I look at my
little clock. Five-ten. Nearly an hour.

Then the crossbar is thrown, and I hear a screw
pattering down the gallery. He stops at my door and
unlocks it.

"Get your stuff together," he says. "You're moving out."

My heart gives a great bound. "Unconditional release" flashes like white lights across my mind.

My voice trembles as I ask, "Am I going out?"

"Naw. You're moving to the ground floor."

His words are like a dash of ice water. To the
ground floor. I know what that means. I have been
denied a parole for a long time—possibly eighteen
months. . . . Stacey, is there no hope of help from
you?

I stow my belongings in my new cell, and look out
desolately at the inmates on the cots in front of me.
They are a crummy-looking lot. Eighteen months.
They will probably drive me crazy during the next
year. No, eighteen months. They will steal my stuff
while I am at work; they will snore and keep me awake;
they will whisper among themselves, and the sound
will be maddening. Eighteen months.

And then the screw is at my cell door with the
parole envelope. I accept it, and hold it fearfully in
my hands. The screw, a new man to me, says, "Well,
open it up. See whatcha got."

I lick my lips. They are parched and my tongue too is dry. My cheeks seem unnaturally cold, but I am afire inside. My hands tremble. My mind is a jumble. My thoughts are like the flashing on and off of a bright light.

Then I have the envelope open, and my fingers are unfolding the slip of paper. Words jump at me . . . I feel my insides drop away. Slowly I pick out the lines of the message. Each word stands starkly against the white.

After considering your application for parole, we must inform you that your case has been continued five years.
State Board of Parole.

I slump down onto my cot.

The screw says, "Well, whadja make?"

I turn from him, and he moves on. I feel the eyes of the men on the cots peering at me. I look out at them. They raise inquisitive eyebrows. I hold up five fingers. They shake their heads.

Suddenly the enormity of my continuance smites me full force. Five years. Five long, dreary years of silence. Five summers and winters and falls and springs.

Five years . . . God, oh, God!

21

You sit here on the cot in your narrow little cell and try to forget that those sounds drumming through the windows are made by birds and wind and free men. You try to stifle thought of the thousands and thousands of miles of open road that lie beyond the walls; you strive to close your mind to them utterly, to forget that you ever traveled their lengths, but you cannot. For too many years they were a part of you. They hover perpetually on the surface of your mind, dimly seen, wavering, brightening and fading, tantalizing you, like a mirage above a desert. And as you stare coldly at the wall of your cell and contemplate the years which lie ahead, your spirit faints. . . . The miles of open road are far away; they are a part of another world; they are beyond you. . . . Ah, freedom, how precious you are!

And there are your flatulent fellow inmates—you'd like to forget them too. But you cannot. They press too closely upon you. Their cots bank the wall of the corridor in front of your cell—a long, endless line, closely packed, that extends entirely around the crowded cell hall. You feel the inmates' eyes eternally upon you, absorbing you—dull, prying eyes. The stares, the snores, the grunts, the midnight cries and moans, the animal noises great and small—all press upon you,

251

day after day, night after night, enraging you, destroy-
ing you as the germs of madness gnaw at your brain.
At times you feel that anything, even death, would be
better than this.

No, you can't forget your fellow inmates, your rest-
less, disintegrating fellow inmates. For you feel yourself disintegrating too. · And you blame them, rather
than yourself, for your mental and moral decay. You
resent everything they do, every movement they make,
even though in most cases they are merely duplicating
your own actions. You have lost all semblance of tol-
erance. You feel rage rather than pity when the con-
sumptive on the third gallery hacks quarter-hourly.
He sounds as if he is slowly strangling, and you hope
in your heart that his next cough will be his last. You
wish to scream or curse or throw yourself violently
against the bars when the thud of hard heels clacking
against a cell floor tells you that the man in 218 is
again trying to pace his mind and body into nerveless
exhaustion.

You listen, grinding your nails into your palms . . .
Thud, thud, thud. Pause. Turn. *Thud, thud, thud.*
Over and over and over. You crouch tensely on the
edge of your chair, and struggle to center your mind
on anything but that maddening rhythm. And then it
stops, and you hunch your shoulders and ball your fists
and sit in an agony of suspense as you wait for the
pacing to start all over again. A minute, an hour, and
then—*thud, thud, thud.* Pause. Turn. *Thud, thud,*

thud. You bury your head in your arms and try to smother the flame of violence that roars within you. . . . And suddenly you realize that you are slipping. You raise your head and look at your hands. They tremble. Your face is wet. Your muscles are knotted, your brain afire. You're all shot to hell. The joint has got you.

"Fellow inmates!" you whisper. "Good Christ!"— You have been whispering a lot since you visited the board room last week . . . whispering to yourself . . . talking aloud sometimes—looking in the mirror and talking. . . .

And then there are the months which lie behind— you don't forget them either. You'll never forget them—never be able to—no matter how hard you try. Drunk or sober, asleep or awake, those months will always live and march, like ghastly blank red masks, across your mind.

You stare at the wall and think, "Over a year gone! One whole, dragging year. Two springs wasted— two springs and a winter and a fall and a summer. Fifteen months in prison . . . Why, even a minute can seem like a long time. But fifteen months——"

And you concentrate on how long a minute can really be. Sixty seconds. You count slowly to sixty—slowly, as your clock tolls off the seconds. One . . . two . . . three . . . And after an eternity, you reach sixty. A minute. But it seemed endless. . . . And then you recall the hundreds of thousands of minutes you've been waiting. A false courage arises.

Your whole situation suddenly appears tragically funny.

What's a minute! What's a million minutes! What's a hundred million billion minutes! You've got all the time in the world! You're all shot to hell anyway. And who cares! It's your life, isn't it? You can kick it away if you want, can't you? Hell, yes.

But your new courage ebbs, and a wave of futility floods over you, as you remember that the long wait isn't over yet. Not by a damn sight it isn't. You're going to wait some more too.

So you try to stifle all your unhappy thoughts in a fury of activity. Maybe you get up, like the man in 218, and attempt to walk yourself into exhaustion. You take three steps toward the rear of your cell, pause and turn by the washbowl, and retrace your steps . . . *Swish, swish, swish.* Pause. Turn. *Swish, swish, swish.* Again and again and again. And your movement is almost silent. You wear rubber heels . . . Why doesn't the guy in 218 wear rubber heels? He's making the same wages as you. Probably saving up his thirty-five cents a day. Getting a tin-horn's bankroll, so some cheap little whore can roll him the first night he's out. The kind of guy that doesn't brush his teeth, and wears the cheap underwear and socks the state furnishes, and uses state soap, and chews state tobacco. Even wears hobnailed state shoes. Won't spend a cent. Blah! The goddam farmer! The cheap yokel son-of-a-bitch! You catch yourself. One year ago, you hardly ever swore. Now you even swear when you think . . . *Swish, swish, swish.* Pause. Turn. Up and down. Up and down. Up and down.

Then perhaps your legs begin to ache, and you're hot and sweaty, and your head feels numb, so you sit down on your cot and wish you had something to read, or some paper to scribble on. So you do the next best thing and dig your playing cards out of your steel wall locker and start a game of solitaire. The nervous little Irishman on the cot directly in front of your cell sits up and eyes you. He has no cards, and must play through your hands.

You lay out the pasteboards, seven piles of them, then count out the cards, three at a time, purposely refraining from making the correct plays. The little Irishman watches you and starts fidgeting because he can't voice his opinion of the way the cards should be played. So you continue to irritate him with your misplays, and he fumes and sputters and keeps looking toward the screws at the center of the cell hall and up on the galleries, hoping, no doubt, that they'll all go to the other side of the building at once so he can tell you how to play your cards. But the screws stay on, and you continue to misplay, and the Irishman rages inwardly, making furtive hissing noises as he paces up and down in front of your cell. And finally he can bear no more, and returns to his cot, and holds his head in fury. Then you smile at him angelically and put away the cards. You even feel a little better. In his irritation, your own woes have submerged themselves for a moment.

Then you sit on your chair and put your elbows on your knees and cup your cheeks in your hands and gnaw at your lips and stare at your shoes . . . What the hell. Fifteen months gone, and more to go. Fifteen months—— But they're all done and over. You'll never get them back. It's the future that keeps you awake nights, talking and whispering, worrying, planning, hoping, scheming, despairing, and, sometimes, very nearly praying. The future taunts you. If you dwell upon it too intensely, the blood starts throbbing in your wrists, pulsing in your throat, pounding in your temples . . . When are you going home? How long will this go on? You don't know. You're even getting to the point where you don't give a damn. And anyway the board will probably give you two or three more years when you see them again. Maybe you'll have to do the entire twenty years. . . .

But what are you going to do with yourself when you are eventually released? By that time nobody'll ever believe you were framed. You'll be just another ex-con. And who'd want an ex-con when plenty of good men with fine records could be had? . . . Change your name. Move to another state. Move far away to another country. Australia. Venezuela. The South Seas. The last frontier. Ah, there is the place for a man like you. The last frontier, where no questions are asked and a man is just what he shows himself to be.

You start from your daydream. No, that running and hiding business never works. And the pioneers forged past the last frontier years ago. If you run away from your past, it will catch up with you sooner or later, and then there'll be hell to pay—worse than if you stuck it out at home. . . . Home! Chances are nobody there'll even talk to an ex-con. So what are you going to do? What's to become of you? After this, what next? . . . It doesn't matter. There are too many years stretching ahead.

You flop down on your cot and tense your muscles to shake off the ache that your former pose started in your back. You listen to the pounding of your little clock . . . God, how slowly the time passes. Only an hour gone. But the birds have hushed; the windows commence to darken;_there is only the whisper of outside traffic passing the prison, and the sigh of the wind, and the animal noises of fifteen hundred convicts.

The future—"Jesus, Jesus, if you're really up there watching over us, if all that stuff the preacher hollers about is true, why don't you help me? I haven't committed any crime, but I'm getting scared. I think I'm going to die soon or go crazy. And I'm still young. I want to live again, and be a normal human being, like everybody else—a man who can talk when he pleases, and carry a box of matches in his pockets, and smoke real, tailor-made cigarettes, and sit by the fire in the evening, and go walking by the lake. . . . I'm too young to die or go crazy. . . . Please, Jesus, help me."

No good. No answer. You only feel worse, more
forlorn and despairing. So you sit up and look at
the cot-dwellers in front of your cell. And you see
a five-time loser—a thief and a rapist all his life—
down on his knees beside his cot, head bowed before
a big picture of the Saviour, crossing himself, praying. . . . Yesterday, while you were working in the
twine plant, he sneaked into your cell and stole your
new bar of soap. Tomorrow, if you forget to lock
your wall cabinet, he'll get your tobacco. But tonight
he's praying. . . . Maybe he's going nuts too. . . .

You fall back on your cot, your mind like a blur
of lights on a wet pavement. You've served too much
time. You've slipped pretty far. You're stir-nuts already, and there's still a lot of time to do. But fifteen
months are gone from your life. . . . You look at the
little clock. How many times will the hour hand swing
around before you go home? You blink unhappily
and close your eyes.

The bell rings three times. Nine o'clock. You
have got through another day. So you pull yourself
up and fumble around for your stub of pencil, and
draw a line through the date on the calendar. You
know it's bad business to keep track of the days that
way, but you do it regardless. The time passes doubly
slowly, but you have a concrete realization that time
is actually passing, that you are really that much closer
to freedom, though time appears to stand still. . . .
And perhaps you ponder a moment over how many
days you have left to do if you must serve the entire

sentence. But you abandon the thought in panic. The result would be too overwhelming.

You make up your bed, brush your teeth, wash your hands and face, and take off your clothes. You slide beneath the blankets, wishing you rated sheets. You have to wear your underwear to bed, and it feels hot and sticky. . . . But some day you'll be sleeping in pajamas again, on a deep, soft mattress, between clean sheets. Silk pajamas, too, by God. . . . Some day.

You lie flat on your back, your hands clasped behind your head, and stare up at the ceiling and think—think: that letter you got from Mother today; the visitors that passed through the shop this morning, and the pretty girl who stared at you as if you were some wild animal; the man who dived off the fourth gallery yesterday morning, and bashed his brains all over the corridor in front of your cell; the little girl who used to live next door so long ago. What was her name? Mayme or Clara or something . . . Wonder what started you thinking about her? Life's funny. . . .

And then the lights go out. Fifteen hundred men sigh and stretch and thrash about. A cricket sings outside the window. A screech owl pitches its thin, high note. Someone starts to snore. So you close your eyes and turn your face to the wall. Another day has slipped into the past. . . . Soon you'll dream and live again, but with the dawn, once more you'll die.

22

WE FILE into the prison yard for our first Saturday afternoon of recreation this year. The snow is gone; the poplar trees beyond the wall once more are a mist of green; and in the nook formed where the north cell hall joins the wall, the sun is warm and bright. Just a year ago, Mueller, Lassiter and I sat here on the grass. Now only I am left. . . . For five years, perhaps more, I shall come to this corner each spring and sit on the warm grass and remember.

I look at the long arm of the solitary cell hall projecting out into the center field of the baseball diamond. . . . Stacey, Stacey—what happened? . . . My request for a visit with Stacey was indignantly denied by the deputy warden. And Lockhart has called on neither Joyce nor me.

Fargo Red, Seiver, Dale and Elman cut across the grass and approach me.

Red says, "Tough luck, Frank. Five years is a hell of a long time."

I say, "Maybe something'll turn up—maybe the pardon board'll give me a break when I apply again."

"Pardon board!" snorts Dale angrily. "You still believe in Santa Claus after the way that lousy parole board treated you?"

260

"Well, I've got to keep myself going some way, even if I don't really believe it."

"Come on along with us, Frank," urges Red. "It's set for breakfast time Tuesday morning."

I shake my head. "No, I haven't heard from the attorney yet. Stacey found Limpy Julien in Los Angeles just before he was picked up on that bank job. The lawyer's men were going after him. They may have learned something."

"Stacey!" snorts Red. "You gotta stop kidding yourself he's gonna get you out. He's tucked away for all time now. And if his lawyer knew anything, he'd of told you by this time."

"I wouldn't go along on the break, anyway, Red. It's pure suicide, and if I want to kill myself, I can do it a lot easier and with a lot less trouble in my cell after lights out. . . . You haven't got a chance."

"Chance!" growls Dale. "We'll be packing a flock of .45's, and anytime we've got a batch of them babies on us, it's the other guy that ain't got no chance."

Elman says, "Come on along, Ross. There ain't very many of us, and we need all the regulars we can get."

"Nope, I don't want to stay here any more than you, but I don't want to get mixed up in a killing and do the book in the hole. Life's a lot more time than five years."

"Maybe it ain't only five years, Frank," reminds Red. "They may sling another five at you when you go up to the board again."

But the threat doesn't register. The time is too far distant, the present too painfully real. I shake my head.

"Fer God's sake, Frank," grumbles Red in aggravation, "git wise to yourself. Come along with us. You'll be outta this joint Tuesday morning, and you'n me'll scram to another country and nobody'll ever find us."

"Nuts. They'd find me all right—dead in the dining hall or out here by the wall. You're walking right into your death. And if you should happen to get away—something a lot of smart men have tried to do and died trying—you'll just be brought back, like Stacey. . . . You lifers—I don't blame you for trying. You've got everything to gain and nothing to lose. I'd try it myself if I were doing the book. But Red—he only got a year from the board, and he's a cinch to get a discharge next spring. He's gambling the rest of his life rather than do a lousy ace, when he's already got in over eight years."

"I can't help it, Frank," says Red. "I can't do no more time. I got to the point where I either gotta git some free air or croak. I'll go screwy as a bedbug if I stay around here any longer. So I'm gonna lam with the boys. And we ain't going over no wall, if that's what you think. We're gonna walk right out the front gates and climb in cars and be drove away so fast it'll make your head swim."

"You'll never get those turnkeys to open the gates," I point out.

"That's what you think," says Dale. "But you never stopped to figure we might throw guns on the deputies right in the dining room and tell them to march us through the gates and into cars or we'll bump 'em right on the spot."

"You wouldn't try a kid stunt like that?" I gasp. "Nearly every time it's been tried in other stirs it's failed."

"Like hell," says Dale. "It's sure fire. I led a break like that in Chelan pen, and it worked like a charm."

"It might work with a yellow deputy warden, but it won't work with Armstrong and Craigie and Pollard. Those guys are tough. They'd die ten times before they'd order the turnkeys to open the gates. . . . Why, that guy Craigie was an ace during the War. He shot down seven German planes, and was shot down twice himself."

"So what," growls Seiver. "The War's over till we start another one."

"You're crazy, Frank," says Red. "The joint's getting you. We can't miss." He pauses a moment and dolefully chews his tobacco. Then, "Think it over, kid. I hate t' think of leavin' you here. We're pals, God damn it."

"I know, Red, but I don't want to go out that way— have to spend the rest of my life on the dodge. . . . And besides, what'll you do if the deputies refuse to open the gates?"

"We'll croak the bastards an' all the rest of the screws," growls Dale.

"And do the book in the hole, or get sent to the nut house like Mueller," I add.

"Well, are you coming or ain't you?" demands Dale, showing impatience.

I'm getting no place with arguments. They're going to make one desperate try, and there's nothing more I can do about it.

"I've been telling you all the while I won't go in on it."

"And here," mourns Red, "I was countin' on you t' go partners with me on the outside."

Each bids me a solemn good-by. I make one last plea to Red. "Try to remember how ninety-nine out of every hundred breaks end," I conclude.

"No use, Frank. I'm going in on it."

"Okay, Red—fellows."

As I stumble across the prison yard, I hear Red saying, "Don't worry none about him. He'll come along when he sees how swell everything's going."

"Throw a gun on him Tuesday and make him come along," snorts Dale. "He's stir-nuts and don't know what he's doing."

That's a pleasant picture for me to mull over until next Tuesday.

In my cell, when we file in from the yard, is a letter from Joyce. I test it for invisible writing. The words form between the lines as I heat the paper with my pipe.

Lockhart 'phoned long distance from Los Angeles today.   Couldn't talk over the 'phone, but he has something.   Be brave, my darling.   He'll be here Monday morning.

Monday morning—the day before the riot.   And perhaps he'll have some good news for me, though I'm sure he'd have told Joyce if he knew anything definite.

I answer the letter Sunday, filling the page with my hopes and aspirations, most of which I had thought dead.   But my biggest regret is being unable to get word of the riot to the paper.   There isn't time.

Monday: The tension has increased hourly.   With the break set for tomorrow morning, Fargo Red is in a continual dither, fearing that he'll do something that will cause him to be thrown in the hole and will then lose his chance to join in the riot.   He's just a big kid.   He's not joining this attempted break because he wants out so much he can't wait a year.   He thinks it's going to be fun—a great change in the deadly, unvarying routine and strict enforcement of the ten thousand childish rules which govern us.

Red watches himself closely.   He doesn't whisper or make signs in the shop today.   At breakfast and during the noon meal he ate everything that was put on his plate.   He hasn't stared at visitors or gazed out of the windows or stayed overly long in the latrine—all offenses which usually cause him trouble. . . .
It will be no fault of Red's if he goes to the hole before hell breaks loose tomorrow morning.

All during the day I've been racking my brain, trying to evolve some plan that will save Red from himself. For, I continually tell myself, I've got to help
him—absolutely must. I can't go to the deputy warden
and snitch on the plotters; the code of the convict for-.
bids that. And the months of imprisonment have
made me a convict in heart and soul. And Red,
blinded by the glamorous thought of holding a smok-
ing gun in his hand and blasting his way out of everything he's come to despise during eight long years,
cannot see reason.

And the time is fleeting—only an hour remains before we shut down the machines and go in for the
night. And then it will be too late. And my pal
Fargo Red will be sunk. . . . He's been my pal for
fifteen months. During that long period, there were
times when only Red's friendship kept me from losing
my mind. I can't forget the crazy and funny things
he'd say, just to snap me out of it when I rocked on
the edge of mental oblivion. I have to help him.

And then, just as I am giving up, I finally see the
one way to save Fargo Red.

I move to the rear of the shop and start opening
bales of sisal with a bale knife. After I've opened
enough to last until long after the machine shuts down,
I drop the knife into my overall pocket, and juggle a
drum of oil over to the oil tank. Then, to avoid any
suspicion, I connect up the hoist and fill the tank.

Now my hands are covered with tarry dirt and
grease and oil from the drum and the tank. I get

permission to wash myself. This entails going to the mop-room sink, and then behind the clothes rack for my towel, which hangs on the hook with my uniform. Red's hook is next to mine. I am out of sight of any of the guards, and in a second the knife is in Red's hip pocket. When the knife is missed during the evening check-up prior to our leaving the shop, every-one will be searched. Then Red's past record for get-ting into mischief and violating the rules should void any protest he'll make.

At last, Mooney blows his tin whistle. We wash, dress, and line up for the count, which is made by Squires while Mooney is at his desk checking up on the knives and pencils used during the day, and Lord, the other guard, is watching the inmates so they can't pass contraband.

"One knife missing," calls Mooney. "Ross, go back and see if it's stuck in a bale or on the floor."

I return to the rear of the shop, pretend to be search-ing diligently, and then report no knife left behind.

Mooney tells Squires and Lord to start searching the inmates. No one thinks anything is amiss, for knives have disappeared before and then turned up the next day under a bale of sisal. But, as a pre-caution against any weapons' being taken into the cell hall, the inmates must be searched before they can leave the shop.

I take my place in the line. Squires' hands frisk me expertly. He moves back to Red, whose place in line is directly behind me. And then it happens.

"Here it is, Mooney."

"Who had it?"

"Red."

A cruel gleam sets in Mooney's eyes as he approaches the hairy man. The guard has hated him for a long time—ever since, eight years ago when Red first came to prison, Mooney interfered in a fight that Red was having with three other inmates and struck Red on the head with his cane. Red broke the cane and threw the pieces in Mooney's face. He still carries the scars.

"Hiding a knife, hey?"

"It's a bum rap!" cries Red, his face tense and angry. "I wouldn't be sucker enough to cop no knife outta here. Somebody planted it on me."

"You'd be sucker enough to try to pull anything," says Mooney. "You need another dose of that hole. . . . Get over against the wall."

"You ain't sending me to the hole on nothing like this. I been framed."

"Get over against the wall."

"The hell with that noise. I ain't done nothing."

"Okay," says Mooney, pleased. "It'll go just that much tougher for you then. . . . Squires, take him over to the deputy, now. I'll make out the report and turn it in on him after the men have been fed."

Squires puts his hand on Red's shoulder and pulls him out of line. "Come on, Fargo. Don't be a fool and make things any tougher than they are," he says in a low voice.

Red .is so bewildered and angry that he can't keep the tears back.

"But I didn't take no knife. Somebody went and planted it on me."

"Tell it to the deputy," grunts Mooney. "He's liable to believe you. . . . Now will you get going, or will we put the iron claw on you?"

Red eyes me sadly. He shuffles his feet, and his whole big frame seems to sag. A trickle of tobacco juice seeps from one corner of his quivering mouth.

"Kin I give Ross my tobacco and stuff?"

"Make it snappy then and get the hell along before the whistle blows."

Red hands me his plug of tobacco, a can of Velvet and a salve box. He blinks hard, and two great tears roll down his cheeks and splash on the front of his coat.

"Somebody framed me, kid. See if you can find him while I'm gone."

I nod. Red gulps, and gives me one last, sad look. . . . Oh, Red, you poor, dumb, trusting pal—if I could only tell you and make you see. Red——

Squires leads him from the shop. I put the plug and the Velvet in my pocket, and open the salve box. A roach scampers around excitedly. . . . I replace the lid, and look down at my shoes, and hope I don't start crying.

23

Tuesday morning, and no word from Lockhart.
The gong clangs four times. We slide open our cell
doors and file to the dining hall, where we take our
seats, fold our arms, and, with eyes held rigidly to the
front, wait for the gong to sound. Armstrong glances
at his pocket watch, replaces it, then nods to the inmate waiter who stands at the bell cord. Bong! Knives
and forks start to rattle.

I glance to my right and left. Everything seems
as it has always been, save that Johnny Carr, who sits
beside me, crouches tensely, as though about to spring
at the first person who passes his table.

Armstrong stands at the front of the dining hall.
Pollard, his first assistant, is at the left of the room;
Craigie, the second, is on the right. Guards are sprinkled up and down the aisles . . . Dale has worked
smoothly and quietly. Not more than two dozen inmates know that hell will be popping in a few minutes. . . .

I'll have to have something definite planned for myself when the trouble starts, for I've been seen talking
and fraternizing with the leaders. Guards and the
rats will remember that and speak of it after the riot
is over. And questions will be asked. Because of the
Stacey affair, I'll be under double suspicion whether

270

I'm in on the break or not.   I must have an iron-clad alibi.

And then there's Dale and his suggestion they throw guns on me and make me come along.   If that were to happen, I could never in the world convince the authorities I was not involved.

I lay out a plan—one which I've been working on ever since Saturday.   As soon as Dale and his pals go into action and have left the dining hall, I'll slide out of my seat, beat it to my cell, and slide the door shut so I'll be locked in.   That will be safer than being in the dining hall with the inmates who don't join. For if I stay there, the warden is likely to believe that I tried to get away with the rioters, but retreated to the dining hall when I saw that the escape was frustrated.   My cell is the only place to which I can go and be free of suspicion.

The waiters thread their way up and down the aisles, rattling big spoons against the sides of their pails of potatoes and thick, greasy gravy.   The meat passers dole out one small piece of pork fat to each inmate. Dale holds out his plate for seconds.   The waiter is Schaefer, a notorious rat who works in the kitchen and has the best interests of the prison at heart.   He sneers and passes on.   Dale jumps from his seat.

"Come back here with more meat, you rat bastard!" he yells.

It is as if I've suddenly gone deaf.   The dining hall is a vast, silent vacuum.   Everyone stares in horror at Dale.   Schaefer stands frozen for a moment.   Then hell breaks loose.

Dale throws his plate into Schaefer's face.   Schaefer starts to run.   The guards bear down on Dale. Men immediately spring up all over the dining hall. They draw guns.   The guards halt in terror.   Never before has a gun been brought beyond the gates of Stony Point.

Johnny springs up beside me.   His pistol booms with a deafening roar, Schaefer sags across a table, strewing the dishes and food on the floor.

Johnny cries, "I got that son-of-a-bitch anyway!"

Dale, O'Brien, Lewis and Elman swarm down on the deputies.   Each of the inmates is armed.   Dale takes charge.   The little man spins the deputy around and slams him against the wall.

"Now," cries Dale, "we're giving the orders around here!"

Armstrong yells, "You fool!   You're digging your own grave!"

"You do as we say or you're digging yours!"

"Put up those guns, you men!" roars the deputy. "You'll never get away with this!"

Dale slugs the deputy with the gun.   A cut opens over his eye.   He sags momentarily, then recovers.

"All right, guys," yells Dale.   "Round up all the screws, and lock 'em in cells. . . . Come on, the rest of you; we'll take these babies down to the gates."

He kicks the deputy warden, shoves a gun into the back of his head, and starts him from the dining hall.

Elman, Seiver, O'Brien and Lewis push the two assistants ahead of them. Johnny Carr and four or five other armed rioters herd the officers together and march them from the dining hall.

Johnny turns at the door and howls, "Come on, all you birds! Anybody wants out, follow us." He waves his pistol wildly.

About two hundred men spring into the aisles with a yell. Prominent among them are the long-suffering cot-dwellers and the inmates from Mad Dog Mooney's shop. All race with fanatic zeal toward the front gates.

I wait a few moments, then start for the north cell hall. But as I swing into the long hallway that leads to the rotunda, I hear firing from the front gates. Someone screams in pain or fright. I hurry, hoping to be able to get into the cell hall before the firing becomes general and cuts me off.

Then someone spies me, yells my name, and Dale is beside me.

"Good boy!" he cries. "We need you with us. Everything's going swell."

"What happened. Who got shot?"

"Mooney. He started hollering for help. Elman got him."

"Where're the deputies?"

"We gave them a couple minutes to make up their minds whether they're gonna take us out the gates or get killed."

"My God, Dale, you look like a crazy man. . . . What's come over you?"

The little fellow grins evilly.   "Come on."

I shake my head.   "Where're the turnkeys?"

"Hiding in the mail room."

"Won't they come out and open up?"

"They'll damn soon do it when they find out we're gonna bump the deputies."

The inmates mill about the gates—two hundred howling, wild-eyed men.   Deputy Armstrong and his two assistants tower above the center of the mass. On their faces is grim determination.   Death holds no fear for them. . . . Dale grabs my arm.

"Come on.   Let's get going."

Before I can refuse, a scuffle breaks out in the center of the mob.   A pistol booms; the rioters scream frenziedly and scuttle crab-like for safety.   Elman is on the floor; Assistant Deputy Pollard has a gun and fires into the fleeing mob.   Then Seiver's .45 jumps, and the officer's face disappears.   He drops on top of Elman.   An inmate grabs the gun from Pollard's dead hand.   The pack closes in again, howling and screaming as though maddened by the sight and taste of blood.   They throw Armstrong against the gates.

"God, Dale, they've killed one of the deputies!" I breathe.

Dale speeds into the mob.   In a moment he is back.

"Pollard snatched Elman's gun and killed him. . . . Make up your mind, now, Ross.   For the last time, you with us or against us?"

"Neither. I'm going to sit this out.up in my cell."

He swings on me, and for a moment I fear he's going to use his gun. Then he turns and cries to Seiver, "If anybody tries to go in the cell hall, let him have it. Anybody, get me?" He stalks back into the mob.

That is what prison has done to little gray-haired Dale. That is what prison has done to two hundred men who, a few minutes ago, were placid sheep, and who now, like sheep, are following their new leader.

I retreat to the far end of the rotunda and stand with my back to the wall. Dale is talking with Deputy Armstrong. A hush shuts over Dale's backers.

"You'll order the gates open and take us to cars," cries Dale, "or I'll blow your hair all over the ceiling!"

"You haven't got the guts, Dale," says Armstrong. "You know you can't get away with this, and you'll do life in the hole."

"You got about ten seconds to find out whether I got the guts or not."

"Ten seconds or ten years—the answer'll always be the same, Dale."

Someone screams, "Kill the big son-of-a-bitch!"

A hundred voices take up the chant. The men press in, howling and yelling like maniacs.

"Quiet!" screams Dale. "Can that racket!" He lashes out with his fist and his gun at several of the inmates, and the din lessens. Dale shouts through the gates, "Hey, you yellow-bellies in there—if these gates ain't open in ten seconds, we're gonna kill Armstrong just like we killed Pollard! And if they ain't open then, we'll kill every screw in the joint!"

Officer Hultman's scared white face peeps around the door post of the mail room. "Is that right, deputy? Did they kill Pollard?"

"Never mind," roars Armstrong. "Don't open the gates . . . Get on the 'phone. Call the warden."

"I've already called him. He's getting extra help."

Dale grabs the deputy, swings him around, and slams him in the face with the pistol. Blood drips.

"Now," cries Dale, "you're really going to die!"

"I'll be seeing you, Dale."

Seiver knocks down Dale's gun.

"Wait, you fool! What about Stacey and Red? Make Armstrong open the solitary. We ain't gonna leave here while they're in the hole?"

Dale says, "My God, I never even thought about it."

He shoves his gun into Armstrong's side. Seiver takes charge of Craigie.

"Get going for the hole," orders Dale. "You're gonna open up for Stacey and Red."

Armstrong grins whitely. The blood streaming down his face makes a grotesque mask. "Not a chance, Dale."

"You'll get them keys and open up or we'll kill Craigie on the spot."

Craigie says, "Let them shoot. They'll end up by killing us anyway."

Seiver shoves his gun against the back of the second deputy's head. "Shall I let him have it, Dale?"

"You got about two seconds, Armstrong," says Dale.

Craigie stiffens himself. Three convicts grab his arms and grin wickedly. Armstrong licks his lips. Then gunfire rattles from outside the main entrance. Glass in the outside door flies across the outer office.

Armstrong says, "Don't shoot him. I'll open up."

The inmates scream and start firing through the gates into the outer door.

"Step on it," orders Dale.

Seiver pushes the inmates who are holding the officers. "Leggo, God damn it! Go report to Pat." He shouts into the mob, "Johnny Carr! Come on along with us. Pat! Take charge here."

Johnny Carr scuttles out from the howling mass of men; the five start across the rotunda for the solitary.

Dale spies me.

"Hey, you—Ross! Get along here."

I shake my head. "Nothing doing. I'm not in on this."

He levels his gun at me.

"I said get along."

The five stop.

Seiver yells, "You'll get over here if you know what's good for you."

I join them. "What the hell's wrong with you guys? I don't want any part of your riot."

"We get it," snarls Dale. "Wanna let the deputies know you're too good to side in with your buddies."

"No, just that I'm not damn fool enough to make that hole for life."

"Yeah," growls Seiver, "he's probably figuring on hollering for help or something from the cell hall so he can get himself a pardon."

I gasp, "Me! Why, you——"

"Get moving," yells Dale. "We ain't got all day."

We start down the hall toward the deputy's office.

Seiver says, "While we're in there, we can get that Carlisle rat outta D.W. and bump him."

Dale barks something unintelligible and pokes Armstrong in the back of the neck with the gun. "Hurry it up there."

Armstrong says, "Get wise to yourself. Put down those guns and maybe it won't be quite so tough on you."

Craigie says, "You'll never get away with it." Then, to Armstrong, "Don't open up for them."

"Shut up!" screams Dale, "before we let you both have it right here."

"What harm will it do to open up?" says Armstrong. "They can't get away, and it may save your life."

Seiver clubs the second deputy with his gun, and the two officers are silent.

We swing into the anteroom of the deputy's office. Dale and Seiver march them directly to the solid steel door that guards the hole.

"Now, open up," commands Dale.

"The keys're in Temple's desk," says Armstrong.

Johnny Carr gets the keys from the lock box.

Seiver sneers, "We shoulda bumped these guys up in front. We coulda found the keys ourselves."

Dale snatches the keys and unlocks the door.

He orders, "Seiver, stay on guard here. Let us know if anything starts happening up by the gates before we're back."

We enter the solitary-cell hall. Dale starts down the hole side, unlocking each door as he goes along. Inmates pop out and excitedly hurl questions. Then Dale stops, jerks open a door, and Stacey walks out.

He says, "What the hell's up? What's all the racket?"

Dale grabs his hand. "Riot, boy. We're crushing out. We came back for you and Red."

Stacey says, "Jesus!"

Seiver runs in. As the heavy steel door swings open, the staccato clatter of machine-gun fire echoes from the front gates.

Seiver cries, "Dale! They threw gas bombs in through the gates! All the guys run into the north cell hall! Now the national guard's out there with machine guns and gas masks!"

Dale says, "Johnny, lock them deputies up in Stacey's cell."

Armstrong and Craigie enter the cell. Johnny Carr turns the key. Seiver says, "Why not bump 'em right now?"

"Save 'em," says Dale. "We may need 'em later for dickering."

"Get Red out, and let's be going!" cries Seiver.

Johnny starts searching the cells for Red. Seiver opens the door. A rattle of machine-gun fire from the hall. Seiver drops. Dale kicks his body aside and slams the door and locks it.

"The national guard's out in the hall," he says slowly. "Funny thing—I never even thought of them till now."

Stacey grabs Seiver's .45 from the floor. "The game ain't up yet," he states. "We'll make it out, using the deputies for protection."

"Out where?" asks Dale. The little man's face is a death-like gray; all the snap and fire has left his eyes.

"Out the back door here. Those keys fit it." Stacey takes over command. "All we gotta do is open the door, pick the screws off the wall, get some rope from the twine plant, and climb over."

"Okay," agrees Dale. "Let's go."

They surge toward the rear door at the back of the solitary-cell hall. Johnny Carr fits the key and swings back the door. A rattle of rifle fire from the guard towers on the wall. Johnny collapses flat on his face. A thin trickle of blood wells from his mouth. He twitches, rolls on his back, and acts as if he is trying to avoid swallowing the blood. Then he is still. Stacey slams the door. A rain of slugs spatter against the sheet steel.

One of the inmates released from solitary clutches at his arm. He whines, "I think they got me."

Stacey cuffs him aside and kneels above Johnny Carr.

"Take him into a cell," orders Stacey. "He's done."

A couple of lifers who have been locked up for months haul Johnny away.

Dale creeps up to one of the rear windows and peers over the ledge.

He says, "God, Stacey, the national guard's got machine guns set up on the roof of the twine plant and in the guard towers already. . . . I guess we're sunk."

Defeat creeps across Dale's face. Panes of glass tinkle to the floor as a hail of bullets sweeps the windows. I duck around to the side that houses the detention ward and hope that no ricochets get me there.

Stacey cries, "Dale, bring me one of the deputies!"

There is the sliding of a cell door and then Stacey's voice rising again.

"We're holding the whip here. Do as we say or we'll bump you on the spot. Write a note to the warden and tell him if he doesn't call off the soldiers and guards and open the gates in five minutes we're gonna kill you. And then in another five minutes we'll kill Craigie."

Armstrong bellows a protest. "You can shoot right now, then, Stacey, for I'm writing no notes. . . . Besides, you aren't in this yet. I'll forget what you've done so far if you'll hand over your gun and go to your cell."

"Lock him up again, Dale," orders Stacey. Then, "Here, one of you cons. Go around to D.W. and get somebody's pen and ink and write the note."

One of the released men tears around past me and dives into an open cell. He rips a page from the

Bible, scribbles a few lines, and dashes back to the other side of the cell hall.

"Here's your chance to be a hero," says Stacey. "Take off your underwear and carry it over your head and take this note to the warden or whoever's running the show from the twine plant."

"I'll get kilt," cries the inmate.

"You'll be carrying a truce flag, won't you? . . . G'wan, get going before I smack you."

I peer around the corner. One of the lifers steps to the door as Stacey swings it open. But before the flag of truce can be waved, a storm of machine-gun bullets sweeps across the opening. The inmate plunges down the steps. Stacey falls back, clutching his shoulder. Dale slams the door and locks it.

"How bad you hit?" he cries.

"Not bad." Stacey regains his control and stands upright. "Just a nick, I guess."

"What'll we do now?" asks Dale. "Shall I get Red out so he can help us?"

"No. The game's up, I'm afraid. Leave Red in there. No sense in getting him jammed up now."

They duck around the corner. I step up to Stacey. "Why don't you do as the deputy said and go in your cell, Stacey? Then maybe you'll be left out of this."

Stacey grins wearily. The blood from his shoulder is spreading, leaving a big spot. He wipes his face with the back of his hand.

"Hello, Frank. I been waiting a long time to see you. Had a surprise for you."

Rifle butts start hammering on the front door.

Dale says, "They'll be blasting it open pretty soon. We'd better get ready for them."

I say, "Go on, Stacey. The riot's a bust. Get in your cell while there's a chance."

Banging and shouting.

Stacey shakes his head, as though he has heard neither the hammering and shouting nor Dale. "No, that won't do me no good, kid. I'm doing the book, and I've still got that Ludke rap hanging over me. I'd do it all in the hole even if I hadn't got mixed up in this."

"I'll never appear against you, Stacey."

"I know you won't, Frank. But the hell with that. This is the last roundup for Stacey." Machine-gun fire starts pouring into the windows of the north cell hall, where the remainder of the rioters had flown. Stacey continues, "But there's still that unfinished business of yours to take care of, before the soldiers really start turning the heat on us here."

A grenade explodes with a terrific roar outside the front entrance of the cell hall. Dale runs to the door and reports it still holding.

"We'd better hurry," says Stacey. "Well, we got an affidavit out of Limpy before I came back here. He turned state's evidence on the two guys that framed you and the aldermen and the car dealer." He turns to Dale. "Throw your guns on the deputies and lock them up in cells on this side."

Dale scuttles to the other side of the building, and returns with the officers. Stacey and Dale herd them into a cell and lock the door.

I cry, "But who were the guys that framed me, Stacey? Have you found them?"

Stacey grins and eases his wounded shoulder. "You'd be surprised."

Another grenade booms outside the front door. Dale shouts, "It's starting to bulge. Get ready."

Stacey says, "Lockhart was going to file a motion for a new trial with the Supreme Court as soon as he got back here. You'll be sprung in a short while. But I've got that surprise for you first." He takes the keys from Dale. "Come on; we got to find Carlisle's cell."

We search along the corridor. Rifle butts smash and pry at the front door. We hurry, and at last we come to the rat's cell. His face pales and his legs sag when he sees Stacey and me.

Stacey says, "Well, rat, so it's caught up with you at last."

"I ain't done nothing," cries Carlisle. "I don't know what you're talking about."

"Remember what I did to your rat partner?" says Stacey calmly. He is unchanged, unhurried now, unruffled, his face the same old sallow parchment mask. "In about two minutes, you're gonna get the same thing."

"Honest, Stacey—honest to God—I ain't done a thing. It was Ludke snitched on you that time."

Stacey opens the door, gets the rat by the neck and throws him out into the corridor.

"First," says Stacey, "I'm gonna shoot your arms and legs full of holes. Then I'm gonna let you have a .45 right between the eyes."

Carlisle cowers against the bars of a cell. He is half on his knees—half praying. "It was Ludke. Honest to God it was."

"I'm not talking about your snitching on me, rat." Then Stacey screams the last words, "I'm talking about you two framing Ross into this joint!"

The rat starts groveling and whining, but Stacey kicks him to his feet and rushes him to the cell in front of which the deputies are locked.

Armstrong yells, "Stacey, put up those guns and listen to reason! You're sunk!"

"I know it, big boy. I just want you to listen to something this rat's got to say."

He kicks Carlisle. "Start talking."

"Honest, we never framed him! We was in New York when it happened!"

Stacey aims the gun at Carlisle's arm and pulls the trigger. The rat screams and scuttles about the floor, clutching at his arm. Blood soaks through his sleeve.

"Start talking."

"You can't do this to an unarmed man," cries the deputy.

Carlisle moans, "I can't. I don't know——"

Stacey aims the gun again.

"Wait!" cries the rat. "I'll talk!"

Stacey says, "You two deputies'll have to repeat what Carlisle says to support an affidavit. Just remember that what he confesses he's doing without coaching. He knows it himself."

Machine-gun fire rattles against the front entrance.

Dale cries, "They're out there shooting off the lock now! For God's sake, Stacey, the hell with this. Let's get ready."

Stacey brushes him aside.

"All right, rat, start talking, and talk straight." He shoves the gun under the rat's nose.

"But my arm—it's all bleeding."

"We'll take care of you after you spill." The hammering is resumed on the door. Voices shout in the anteroom. "Get going, and make it snappy."

"Me and Ludke framed Ross," sobs Carlisle. "We done it just before we got sent up on this rap." He collapses at Stacey's feet. The bank robber kicks him.

"Who hired you?"

"Limpy Julien hired us for them four aldermen and that car dealer."

"Why?"

"So we'd frame Ross and people wouldn't believe the stuff he'd found out about the graft rackets."

"God damn you!" yells Stacey. "Talk fast and stop skipping things." He lashes at Carlisle with the barrel of the gun.

"I will! I will! We loaded Ross in his car, knocked him out, and poured whiskey down his throat. Then we busted the bottle in the front seat and run the car

into that other one. We got five grand from the aldermen and the car guy; Limpy got two grand."

The front door caves in with a crash. Dale speeds
forward, and his guns start barking.

"Quick!" yells Stacey. "How'd you get off this rap
so easy?"

Words pour from Carlisle's mouth in a torrent as
he fearfully eyes the muzzle of the gun. "We bumped
a guy for another party that wanted to collect the insurance. Then when we all got picked up, we hung
him so he couldn't turn state's evidence. The district
attorney and his assistant Grayce had been getting
theirs from the graft, so when the aldermen and the
car dealer went to them, they made a dicker for five
years for us if we wouldn't snitch on them."

Dale races back. "I held them off for a minute.
They'll be pouring in though."

"No hurry now, Dale." Stacey takes my hand.
"We're square now, kid. So long."

Before I can answer him, he tosses the keys on the
floor and kicks Carlisle to his feet. "Come on, rat.
You didn't think we'd leave you behind to deny that
confession, did you?"

Stacey and Dale haul the screaming rat out of sight
behind the cell block at the rear of the building. A
shot booms out hollowly. Then two others ring out
in quick succession. An ominous quiet settles over
the detention ward. I look around. I am alone.
All the released prisoners have scurried back to their

cells. . . . I pick up the keys and open the door of the cell holding the deputies.

Armstrong says, "That clears you then, Ross."

My ears are singing with "You're going home—you're going home."

Deputy Craigie shouts, "Don't shoot, out in front there! It's Armstrong and Craigie!"

I run to the rear of the building and peer around the corner of the cell block. The bottom of my stomach falls away. . . . I'll never again have to wonder where Stacey is or what he's doing. . . . We're square now, kid. So long. . . .

Through the windows, I see soldiers herding the rioters from the north cell hall and lining them up in the prison yard.

I return to the front of the building.

"All gone?" asks Armstrong.

I nod. "Yes. All gone."

"It was the only way out for them," says Craigie sadly, shaking his head.

They join the soldiers and guards, who congratulate them on being alive. I walk around to the other side of the cell hall and open the oak door to Red's cell.

"Frank!" he cries. "I heard all the shootin'! Did you come t' git me out?"

I eye him sadly. "Yes, Red. I came to get you out. As soon as I confess something to Armstrong, he'll let you out of the hole."

The pass comes for me at noon two weeks later—
just fifteen months and twenty-nine days from the day
I entered prison.   Deputy Armstrong himself leads
me across the hall to the tailor shop and makes me
understand that it's over at last—that I'm going home
now—that I'm being granted a new trial.

"But it's merely a formality," he concludes.   "Your
bond's posted now, so you can go free.   There won't
be any trial.   The D. A.'ll nolle the charge."

"How about Fargo Red?   Is it okay if I see him?"

"Sure.   Come in my office when you're dressed."

"Okay.   I've got something of his I want to return."

I don my own clothes this time—the suit I wore so
long ago when I came to Stony Point.   I get a shave
and a haircut, then go to the deputy's office.   Fargo
Red is sitting morosely on the edge of a chair.   He
jumps up and grabs my hand.

"Ah, gee, kid—so yuh hadda frame your old partner
into the hole to keep him from gittin' hisself killed,"
he gulps, brushing at his eyes.

"Skip it, Red.   There'll be a new administration in
office damn soon now.   Then we'll have you out and
back with your old lady in Fargo."

"God damn it, Frank," sniffs Red, "I guess I ain't
half as tough as I used to be."

"Here's something of yours, Red."   I hand him his
plug, his Velvet and his salve box.   "Take good care
of Herman."

He rattles the box gently, then winks two big tears

down his cheeks. "I can't say no more. Good-by, Frank." He stumbles out into the hall.

Deputy Armstrong says, "Let's go, Ross."

We walk to the gates, where the deputy okays me through. I shake his hand. Then my sadness drops from me, for I'm through the gates, and Joyce is in my arms, and Jerry's speedgun is popping, and Bill and Lew and Joe are pounding my back and leading me out into the bright, fresh sunshine.

I breathe, "Free!"

Joyce's lips are close to my ear. "It's over, darling. Let's never even think of it again."

The chairman of the parole board and Governor Hanley are just entering the prison on business. Jerry's camera clicks. Joe Campbell doffs his hat, bows low, and says,

"Why, Mis-ter Grayce and Your Excellency! Fancy meeting you here!"

The pair ignore him and sweep in the board room. Bill Mason growls, "Yeah, Grayce may think he's still going to put in only those three days a month here with the parole board, but I've got a hunch that it won't be so awfully long before both he and His Excellency'll be working here regular."

Joyce and I stand on the steps with arms around each other.

Joyce says, "Don't even answer, dear. Remember, we've got each other to think of now, and we're going to forget all about this."

I pull her close to me, and the faces of the grinning reporters and the bystanders, the free green world and the bright sunshine merge into a vast, pleasant haze.

Then Joe Campbell barks, "C'mon, c'mon, you birds. Quit stalling. Only five hours till deadline on the fast mail edition, and Ross's got a long story to write."

THE END